Eclipse of Kings
Denis Judd

1 *A military parade in Berlin, showing the Kaiser marching with his six sons.*

Eclipse of Kings

European Monarchies in the Twentieth Century

Denis Judd

BOOK CLUB ASSOCIATES · LONDON

To my parents

Contents

Author's Preface

This book does not set out to provide an exhaustive analysis of the history of the monarchies of Europe during the twentieth century – indeed, there is no section on the British royal family, since I have dealt with this subject in my recently-published *House of Windsor*. What the book tries to do, however, is to focus attention on what seem to me to be the most important personalities, family connections, and events in European royal history since the beginning of the century. There have, of necessity, been a good number of omissions, but I hope that the reader will forgive me for them. Finally, I am grateful for information supplied by the embassies of Austria, West Germany, Norway, Romania, Sweden and Yugoslavia.

Denis Judd
London, 1975

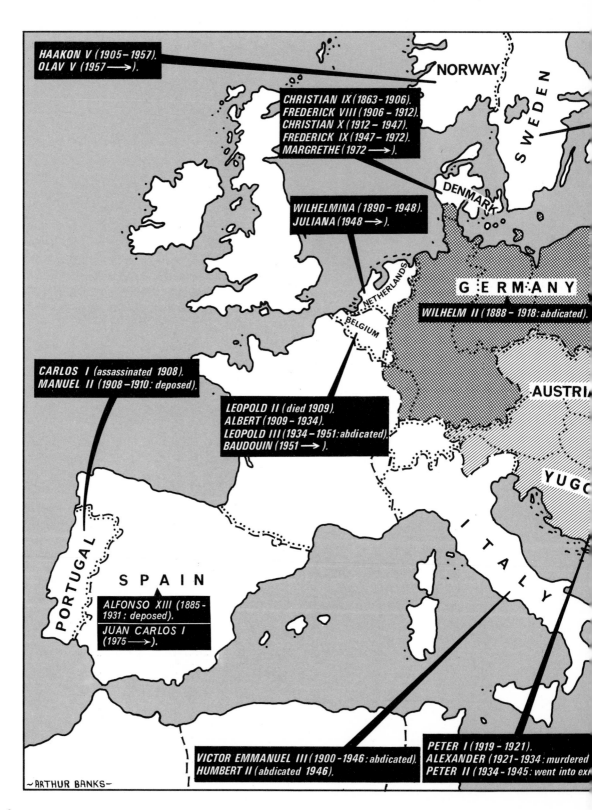

HAAKON V (1905 – 1957).
OLAV V (1957 ⟶).

NORWAY

CHRISTIAN IX (1863 – 1906).
FREDERICK VIII (1906 – 1912).
CHRISTIAN X (1912 – 1947).
FREDERICK IX (1947 – 1972).
MARGRETHE (1972 ⟶).

SWEDEN

DENMARK

WILHELMINA (1890 – 1948).
JULIANA (1948 ⟶).

NETHERLANDS

BELGIUM

GERMANY

WILHELM II (1888 – 1918: abdicated).

AUSTRIA

CARLOS I (assassinated 1908).
MANUEL II (1908 – 1910: deposed).

LEOPOLD II (died 1909).
ALBERT (1909 – 1934).
LEOPOLD III (1934 – 1951: abdicated).
BAUDOUIN (1951 ⟶).

YUGO

PORTUGAL

ITALY

S P A I N

ALFONSO XIII (1885 –
1931: deposed).
JUAN CARLOS I
(1975 ⟶).

VICTOR EMMANUEL III (1900 – 1946: abdicated).
HUMBERT II (abdicated 1946).

PETER I (1919 – 1921).
ALEXANDER (1921 – 1934: murdered
PETER II (1934 – 1945: went into exi

~ARTHUR BANKS~

8

OSCAR II (1872 – 1907).
GUSTAV V (1907-1950).
GUSTAV VI (1950-1973).
CARL XVI (1973 →).

LEGEND
– – – FRONTIERS OF 1914.
········· PRESENT-DAY FRONTIERS.

ROMANOVS
HOHENZOLLERNS
HAPSBURGS

The three monarchies which collapsed as a result of the 1914 war.

R U S S I A

NICHOLAS II (1894 – 1917 : abdicated : murdered in 1918).

FRANZ JOSEPH (1848 – 1916).
KARL (1916 – 1918 : abdicated).

HUNGARY

ROMANIA

BULGARIA

SLAVIA

ALBANIA

GREECE

CAROL I (1881 – 1914).
FERDINAND (1914 – 1927).
MICHAEL (1927 – 1930 : deposed)(1940 – 1947 : abdicated).
CAROL II (1939 – 1940).

FERDINAND (1887 – 1918 : abdicated).
BORIS III (1918 – 1943).
SIMEON II (1943 - 1946 : deposed).

GEORGE I (1864 – 1913 : assassinated).
CONSTANTINE I (1913 – 1917 : deposed).
ALEXANDER I (1917 – 1922 : abdicated).
GEORGE III (1922 -1924 : deposed)(1935 : restored – died 1947).
PAUL (1947- 1964).
CONSTANTINE II (1964 - 1967 : exiled).

ZOG (1928 -1939 : forced into exile).

0   300
MILES

The European monarchs of the twentieth century.

Introduction

The European monarchies of the twentieth century, so many of them linked by blood to Queen Victoria, have been scattered like chaff before the whirlwind of revolution; the gentler breezes of egalitarianism and democratization have sapped their ancient strength, and the chill draughts of indifference and contempt have eroded the primitive mystique of monarchy itself. Two World Wars, many smaller conflicts, economic and social convulsions, political upheavals, and drastically altered habits and conventions have all contributed to the undermining of the concept and practice of monarchy.

At the time of writing, European monarchies are only functioning in Scandinavia, the Low Countries and the United Kingdom. Even these monarchies have made notable adjustments to changed times: Scandinavian and Dutch royalty have taken to their bicycles; heirs to the throne have been educated at State schools; press conferences have been given; television films made; instead of constricting themselves to made-to-measure and expensive clothes, some sovereigns, like their subjects, buy ready-made from chain stores; political 'power' has been surrendered in exchange for an often hazy 'influence'. Even the most prestigious of surviving European monarchies, the House of Windsor, has made substantial concessions to contemporary standards.

Elsewhere, however, European royal houses have been less adaptable, or less fortunate. The First World War destroyed the great triumvirate of Romanovs, Hapsburgs and Hohenzollerns; hardly had these Imperial eagles crashed to the ground than the Ottomans were overthrown. In the period between the two World Wars the Spanish monarchy joined that of Portugal in exile; further east, the Balkan rulers tended to aspire to arbitrary power, and several threw in their lot with Hitler's 'New European Order' – they were, for the most part, rewarded with the establishment of Communist governments, and banishment. The Italian royal house barely survived the fall of Mussolini, and in Greece the monarchy hung on by a thread, only to chance its arm against the despotism of the 'Colonels', to be exiled, and eventually to be decisively rejected in a referendum.

So the exiles have made the best of it, often supported by funds prudently banked abroad during palmier days. Rather like those early Liberal and Radical refugees from nineteenth-century monarchical despotism, the royal fugitives settle in London, or Paris, or Basle, or even Alexandria; they dally in the resorts of the Côte d'Azur, they shoot grouse in Scotland, they journey to the great spas, where once the crowned heads of Europe gathered when the twentieth century was young. Sometimes they can catch a glimpse of past glories when they are invited to a royal wedding – either of a ruling or of an exiled house. But exile or dethronement is not altogether unwelcome to all; rather as fallen cabinet ministers enter into lucrative business partnerships, settle down to read Trollope or write their memoirs, so ex-Kings and their families develop their dormant interests in history or ornithology or, more recently, sociology. Gradually the dispossessed merge into the wealthier classes of their countries of adoption, hopes of restoration steadily fading; when such hopes have faded altogether it is not uncommon to see ex-royalty living within their family's former realms (the Hohenzollerns in Federal Germany, for example) while the representatives of the Napoleonic, Bourbon and Orleanist dynasties of France have lived through a variety of republics.

Despite the century's brilliant opening for Europe's royal houses, their subsequent trials and misfortunes have at least enabled them to share the tribulations of humbler citizens; they have suffered death through war and revolution, they have been victims of social change, they have found their economic circumstances straitened. Though a significant number of thrones have survived, the overall casualty rate has been high; this is not to mourn the passing of unwanted dynasties and archaic privileges, but rather to suggest that even in their darkest hour the monarchies of Europe have come a little closer to the mundane lot of the common man.

Chapter One

Germany: The House of Hohenzollern

The Kaiser Wilhelm II ascended the throne of Imperial Germany on 15 June 1888; he was the third of his house to become Emperor, the ninth to become King of Prussia, and the last to reign over the bustling, dynamic lands that stretched from Poland to the Rhine, and south to the Alps. Imperial Germany was the greatest military power in Europe, and just as the potential of German arms had been brilliantly demonstrated in the recent wars against Austria (1866) and France (1870–1), so the huge economic and industrial capabilities of the German people were also unfolding before envious eyes.

Oddly, at the centre of this ordered, efficient and well-disciplined nation, there was, in June 1888, an atmosphere of suspicion, vituperation and hysterical self-aggrandizement. The new Kaiser, the thirty-year-old Wilhelm II, had seen two Kaisers die since the New Year of January 1888. In March the old Emperor Wilhelm I had died, with dignity, after a life full of the most splendid achievement; in June his son the Emperor Frederick III had finally succumbed, after an heroic struggle, to cancer of the throat. Wilhelm II had mourned his grandfather, but had watched with icy detachment as his father Frederick III, the hope of German liberals, had surrendered his grip on life.

The new Kaiser had resented his father's accession to the throne, and had spent the ninety-nine days of his reign in preparing the way for his own elevation; he had distributed busts and autographed photographs to officials and officers, and had done his best to isolate his hated mother Victoria (eldest child of Queen Victoria). Convinced that his mother was engaged in treasonable contact with Britain, Wilhelm II did not wait for his father's body to become cold before sealing off the New Palace in Potsdam and ransacking the late Emperor's desk for incriminating material. None was found, but the episode provides a striking example of Wilhelm's pathological suspicion and deep-rooted insecurity.

Wilhelm II's neurotic self-assertiveness owed a great deal to the circumstances of his birth. He had been prised from his mother's womb, in an effort to save her life; at first the doctors devoted all their attention to her, and had then noticed in horror that the infant prince lay apparently lifeless beside her. A determined midwife had slapped the baby into life, but within a month it became clear that his left arm and hand, though perfectly formed, were virtually paralysed. In the panic that accompanied his birth, the prince's left arm had been badly damaged at its socket and at the elbow; this limb never matched the other arm in size, and in adult life the hand merely reached the welcome refuge of the jacket pocket.

Wilhelm's withered left arm need not have contributed, in itself, to the crushing feeling of inadequacy which overshadowed his early years. His upbringing, however, had been disastrous; his father was ineffectual and neutral, but his dominating mother had been determined that he would overcome his disability, which in her eyes appeared loathsome and shameful. The unfortunate boy was subjected to a ruthless regime of physical and

3 Four generations of Hohenzollerns at the height of their prestige. At the top, Wilhelm the first Emperor (Kaiser) of a united Germany. Below him, left, his son, the Emperor Frederick III. On the right, Frederick's son, Wilhelm II (the Kaiser of the First World War). At the bottom, his heir, Crown Prince Wilhelm.

intellectual improvement under the cold eye of his tutor Georg Hinzpeter; he had to attempt riding, shooting and drill as if he had no physical handicap whatsoever, and in addition (as he later wrote), 'We tortured ourselves over thousands of pages of grammar, we applied its magnifying glass and scalpel to everything from Phidias to Demosthenes, from Pericles to Alexander, and even to dear old Homer.'

Amid all these trials, Prince Wilhelm made remarkable progress; he was undeniably highly intelligent, learnt to ride more than adequately, and, according to his cousin George V, who was an unrivalled judge in these matters, 'shot remarkably well considering he [had] only one arm'. But to all his achievements his mother was unresponsive, telling his grandmother Queen Victoria disparagingly that Wilhelm had neither 'brilliant abilities nor any other strength of character or talent'. Fortunately his grandmother thought more highly of him, and provided him with some of the love for which he so desperately craved. For his part, he repaid her with an undiluted devotion that sent him, for example, rushing to her side during her last hours at Osborne in January 1901.

In fact, the Kaiser's attitude towards Britain neatly reflected the ambivalence and instability of his character. He loved his grandmother deeply, but entertained an intense dislike of his uncle King Edward VII whose easy-going nature he mistook for urbane condescension; for much of his reign he was a warm admirer of British ways, though he later became passionately anti-British; Herbert von Bismarck, son of the great Otto von Bismarck, noted how Wilhelm 'can never hear enough against England', yet in 1911 the Kaiser told Theodore Roosevelt, 'I adore England!'

The Kaiser's life and reign were riddled with contradictions. Shy, sensitive and intelligent, he fostered the reputation of a ruthless warlord; he hid his insecurities beneath his swaggering self-assertiveness; he glorified himself, strutted and bellowed, and yet could show a charm and consideration that rendered him irresistible; his wife, the docile Augusta Victoria of Schleswig-Holstein-Sonderburg-Augustenburg (known as Dona), bore him six sons and one daughter, yet gossips noted not only his close friendship with the bisexual Count Philipp zu Eulenburg but also his tendency to pat good-looking young officers on the bottom.

For thirty years this able, bellicose, neurotic, but essentially pathetic figure stamped across the European stage, treating an audience that was both fearful and admiring to one bravura performance after another. Typical of his dramatic public pronouncements was his first message on becoming Emperor, when he addressed his army with the words, 'We belong to each other – I and the army – we were born for each other and will cleave indissolubly to each other, whether it be the will of God to send us calm or storm.'

If Wilhelm had been ruler of some petty principality or even of Bavaria, which had harboured the 'mad King' Ludwig II, his eccentricities and his fire-eating speeches would have been of little account. But he was Emperor of a state that had, since unification, enjoyed an unprecedented economic growth; Imperial Germany also plunged into the *fin de siècle* competition for overseas colonies, and, in 1898 and 1900, passed Navy Laws which contained a direct and ominous challenge to British naval supremacy. Yet Germany was not a true constitutional monarchy, for the Kaiser could influence, and dismiss, his ministers in a way far beyond the wildest dreams of Queen Victoria or her successors.

Within two years of his accession to the throne, Wilhelm II screwed up sufficient courage to force the resignation of Bismarck, Imperial Germany's 'Iron Chancellor'. There followed a succession of eight Chancellors during Wilhelm's reign, of whom the most well-known are Bernhard von Bülow and Theobald von Bethmann-Hollweg. None of them matched the legendary Bismarck in statesmanship or in ability to control the Reichstag (the German parliament). But, of course, there was a masterful and vigorous helmsman now steering the Imperial ship of state! The Kaiser's dramatic interventions in the fields of foreign and domestic policy became notorious, and were justly resented by his long-suffering ministers. His involvement in affairs of state would have mattered less if he had practised consistency and moderation, but, alas, this was quite beyond him. He had no fixed policies, no sober personal philosophy to give him direction, and, as he lurched from one initiative to another, the ship of state lurched with him.

The Kaiser's reign was marked by frenzied royal activity and considerable ostentation. He scrapped the frugal court life that had characterized his grandfather's reign, and began to display himself as the glittering Emperor of a glittering Imperial nation. His main residence was the Berlin Palace, and its 650 rooms were bustling with courtiers, guests and servants. In one day a gargantuan amount of food would be consumed in the palace, and Wilhelm had sixty other palaces scattered round his domain. He became an indefatigable traveller, and a luxurious royal train, with twelve carriages, was kept in constant readiness. His travels became, in fact, a joke, when they were not matters for controversy. Though his grandfather had been called 'the wise Emperor' (*der weise Kaiser*), he was nicknamed 'the travelling Emperor' (*der reisende Kaiser*); it was also suggested that Germany's anthem 'Hail to Thee in Victor's Laurels' (*'Heil Dir im Siegerkranz'*) should now be entitled 'Hail to Thee in Thy Special Train' (*'Heil Dir im Sonderzug'*). Wilhelm also had an Imperial yacht built, the *Hohenzollern*, at a cost of 4,500,000 marks. In the wake of his peregrinations he scattered an embarrassing volume of richly ornamented decorations and mementoes – diamond-encrusted Orders of the Black Eagle, gold-framed photographs of himself, silver breast-pins, gold watches and chains. He travelled in a solid gold helmet, and sported an amazing variety of uniforms, many of which he had personally designed.

Of course Wilhelm busied himself with affairs of state too, but he did so erratically. The day began briskly enough when he rose at 6 a.m., in the Hohenzollern tradition established by Frederick the Great, and began work after taking coffee. But his attention to his paper work was at best fitful; he hated long letters and documents and often threw them into the wastepaper basket (a sad contrast to Queen Victoria, earnestly plodding through her state papers); he barely read the newspapers, though he did look at selected and generally inoffensive cuttings; dispatches and memoranda he skimmed through and decorated with marginal comments that were, for the most part, shallow, and sometimes absurd.

Desk work was not the Kaiser's forte. Dressing up, however, was: he had some civilian clothes for country wear, and donned tweeds when he played the English aristocrat on his visits to Britain; but his main passion was for uniforms. Admittedly there was a Hohenzollern tradition that uniforms were the work-clothes of the family, but Wilhelm carried it to excess. Several tailors were permanently in residence at court, making new uniforms and adapting old ones. The Kaiser had uniforms for every occasion, for visiting each of his regiments, for receiving foreign dignitaries, for travelling abroad, for inspecting the fleet, for wearing at court, for informal use. Wags, indeed, claimed that he even had a special admiral's uniform for his visit to the opera to see *The Flying Dutchman*. His wife, the Empress Augusta, was also robed as gorgeously as possible. All the efforts of the royal dressmakers could not, however, transform patient, dull Dona into a fashionable mirror of the age. She looked, so a despairing court official thought, 'like any simple, middle-class girl from the provinces'. To do her credit, the Empress deplored lavish spending on clothes, preferring instead to endow new churches in Berlin.

The Kaiser also dressed in style for his sporting activities, which were numerous and occasionally barbaric. Doubtless the rigour with which he pursued his pastimes was meant to show the world that a withered arm was no deterrent to a variety of activities. In particular, he exulted in the slaughter of animals during the hunt. One of his specialities, in fact, was the lengthy stabbing to death of a wild boar (or, so the sceptics thought, a wild sow) with a ceremonial sword called a *Saufeder*; basking in the applause vouchsafed him after this performance the Kaiser would hand the *Saufeder* to a specially honoured spectator. Not all onlookers were exhilarated by the Kaiser's part in this exhibition, and one of his court officials referred to it as a 'disgusting and degrading spectacle'.

Wilhelm had other talents. He enjoyed yacht racing at Cowes. He could sing a pleasant baritone, and even tried his hand at composing an opera, *Der Sang an Aegidia* ('Song to Aegidia'), which he insisted that the Royal Opera should perform, though the critics were cool in their reception of the lavish production. He painted and designed – especially elaborate uniforms; he also enjoyed card games, though only if he won. Convivial in a boorish fashion, he developed a particularly unpleasant habit of turning inwards the stones of the many rings on his right hand so that he could crush and hurt the hands that he shook.

It was natural that so insecure a man would find enemies on all sides. At home, he detested the Social Democrats and disliked the Jews – though wealthy members of that faith were tolerated at court. The Social Democrat vote, however, continued to grow during his reign, much to his distress. The Kaiser was particularly sensitive to criticism, even from humble citizens; one good example of this occurred when two small boys were overheard by a policeman to say that their father had called Wilhelm a *Windbeutel* (a wind-bag); their father was arrested and imprisoned for two years.

Abroad there was no lack of foes for the Kaiser. He approached each delicate question of foreign relations not with an open mind but, as one of his biographers has remarked, with 'an open mouth'. He raged at the Franco-Russian alliance of 1894, though he had himself let Bismarck's treaty with Russia lapse after 1890. He sent German troops off to suppress the Boxer Rebellion in China in 1900 with the words, 'No mercy must be shown. No prisoners will be taken. As a thousand years ago the Huns under King Attila made a name for themselves still powerfully preserved in tradition and legend, so through you may the name "German" be stamped on China for a thousand years, so that never again may a Chinese dare to look askance at a German.' He was offended by the French anthem the *Marseillaise*, which he considered to be an anthem for regicides. He called the King of Italy 'the dwarf' and his queen the 'daughter of a cattle thief'.

Towards Britain his attitude remained one of neurotic ambiguity. The devoted grandson of Queen Victoria was cheered when he attended her funeral, yet, with the aid of Admiral Tirpitz, he pushed Germany into second place in the navy league – thus posing one of the most serious threats to British security for a century. He still revelled in social contact with the British royal family and aristocracy, yet supported President Kruger of the Transvaal in 1896 after the ignominious Jameson raid on Boer territory, and told the British people in a remarkable article in the *Daily Telegraph* in 1908 that 'You English are like mad bulls. . . .

You make it uncommonly difficult to remain friendly with England.'

In effect, of course, British policy towards Germany was not liable to violent alteration in response to some unguarded comment of the Kaiser's; none the less British public opinion was periodically inflamed by his tactlessness. Oddly, when the prospect of a general war loomed before Europe in July 1914, the Kaiser was anxious to preserve the peace. But Britain eventually threw in her lot with France and Russia, and the Kaiser exploded into wrathful denunciation: 'So the celebrated *encirclement* of Germany has finally become an accomplished fact. . . . Even after his death Edward VII is stronger than I, though I am still alive . . . our consuls in Turkey and India, agents, etc., must get a conflagration going throughout the whole Mohammedan world against this hated, unscrupulous, dishonest nation of shopkeepers – since if we are going to bleed to death, England must at least lose India.'

The Great War cost Germany the lives of 1,773,700 of its subjects, and wounded and crippled 4,216,058 more; it also brought the House of Hohenzollern crashing down, and erected the Weimar Republic in its place. At first, however, the Kaiser and his nation had closed ranks. Wilhelm had declared that there were no longer any political parties in the Second Reich, only Germans, and the Social Democrats had voted the necessary war credits in the Reichstag. In some ways the war should have provided Wilhelm with his supreme moment, for he was now the unquestioned overlord of the nation in arms, unfettered by tiresome constitutional restrictions. In practice, though, the Kaiser found the responsibilities crushing; he preferred to anticipate enormous victories rather than to supervise them.

Privately, for he was not without insight, he came to doubt whether the war could end in a great German victory – or even in victory at all. Yet he was obliged to strut before his people as the embodiment of martial prowess and national self-confidence. Often his reaction was one of childish self-pity, as when he complained, 'To think that George [George V] and Nicky [Tsar Nicholas II] should have played me false! . . . If my grandmother [Queen Victoria] was alive, she would never have allowed it.' Basically Wilhelm shied away from his role as warlord in the midst of a real war, even though he grumbled to Prince Max of Baden, 'If people in Germany think I am the supreme commander, they are grossly mistaken. The General Staff tells me nothing and never asks my advice. I drink tea, go for walks, and saw wood.' He also found time to rant against his British cousins, saying, in response to the Royal Navy's blockade of Germany, that 'before he would allow his family and grandchildren to starve he would blow up Windsor Castle and the whole Royal family of England.'

The Kaiser's impact on the course of the war was, overall, negligible. He was unwilling to unleash the High Seas fleet upon the Royal Navy and hence, perhaps, break the crippling blockade of Germany, and after the Battle of Jutland in 1916 he ordered the fleet back to the safety of home waters. Towards the end of 1916 he made an unconvincing diplomatic foray aimed at ending the war; but he would not spell out details to President Wilson of the United States, and this peace initiative from the former swaggering warlord simply faded away.

Moreover, from January 1917 Wilhelm passed political control over to the heroes of Tannenberg and the Masurian Lakes, Generals von Hindenburg and Ludendorff. When civilian protests were made the Kaiser proclaimed that 'Politicians hold their tongues in

wartime, until strategists permit them to speak!' Even the authority of the Imperial Chancellor Bethmann-Hollweg crumbled before the military dictatorship of Hindenburg and Ludendorff. As previously, the Kaiser had failed to unite his nation, and in the latter years of the war socialist and Communist agitation spread. He helped to contribute further to his dynasty's collapse when he sanctioned the use of unrestricted submarine warfare, which was a powerful factor in involving the United States in the war – and hence in bringing about the downfall of Imperial Germany.

By August 1918, however, the tide of war had turned decisively against Germany; though Bolshevik Russia had made peace, Ludendorff's great western offensive had failed. Throughout September and October the German leadership struggled to avert revolution, while Hindenburg and Ludendorff assured the Kaiser that military defeat was inevitable and urged an expeditious armistice.

At the end of October it became clear that Austria was ending all hostilities; Prince Max of Baden, now Imperial Chancellor, begged the Kaiser to abdicate so that the monarchy could be saved during the coming peace negotiations; the Social Democratic leaders, men like Ebert and Scheidemann, wanted to transform the House of Hohenzollern into a constitutional monarchy, preferably under a son of the Crown Prince Wilhelm who was disliked at least as much as his father.

But even when Austria and Turkey surrendered at the beginning of November 1918, even when the sailors at Kiel rose in rebellion, and even when socialists had seized power in several of the great German cities, Wilhelm II obstinately refused to abdicate; by so doing he sealed the fate of his House. Finally, as news came through that Bavaria had declared itself a republic and that revolutionary crowds were besieging government buildings in Berlin, Wilhelm agreed to abdicate as Emperor, but not as King of Prussia; Max von Baden, however, simply announced that the former monarch had abdicated as both Emperor and King of Prussia, and that the Crown Prince had renounced the succession.

Events now swept away the last vestiges of hope for the Hohenzollerns; in Berlin, Karl Liebknecht proclaimed a 'Socialist Republic', and Scheidemann a 'Republic'. The ex-Kaiser fled to Holland, angrily justifying his reign and bitterly complaining that (unlike the British) the German people put self before country. As he slumped down to exile in Amerongen Castle, the deflated warlord remarked wearily to his host, 'What I should like, my dear count, is a cup of tea – good, hot English tea.'

In 1920 the ex-Kaiser moved to a comfortable house at Doorn in Holland. The Dutch government courageously and sensibly refused to hand him over to the Allies for 'trial'. Wilhelm was a model exile: he behaved more like an English country gentleman than the ex-Emperor of a great nation; he grew a beard, chopped down innumerable trees, formed a local literary society, and wrote scientific and historical papers. Deeply grieved by the death of the ex-Empress 'Dona' in 1921, he married an aristocratic German widow (Princess Hermine von Schönaich-Carolath), the mother of five children, in 1923. His old age was, in fact, tranquil and happy.

His eldest son, the former Crown Prince Wilhelm, returned to Germany in 1923 where he developed the reputation of a playboy. In 1933 he associated himself with the Nazi party, which two of his brothers (Oscar and Augustus Wilhelm) had already joined in 1931; two of the ex-Crown Prince's sons later joined the party.

The Nazis arguably rose on the ruins of the House of Hohenzollern – for what was the

Führer but a demagogic warlord enjoying devoted mass support? The Kaiser's heirs played an assortment of roles during the inter-war and wartime periods. The 1944 plotters against Hitler's life toyed with the idea of restoring a figurehead Hohenzollern, but other members of the House fought for the German cause, and Prince Wilhelm (the ex-Crown Prince's eldest son) was killed during the invasion of France.

When German armies invaded Holland, the ex-Kaiser refused all offers of hospitality, including one from his British cousins. Instead Wilhelm chose to stay with the Dutch people and not to 'run away' again – something of which he had been accused in 1918. On the other hand he sent Hitler a congratulatory telegram when Paris fell in 1940, thus damaging the monarchist, anti-Nazi cause in Germany. When he died on 4 June 1941, however, the ex-Kaiser left instructions that he was to be buried at Doorn, among his Dutch neighbours, rather than taken back for a state funeral in Germany, something that would have benefited only the Nazis.

When peace was restored in 1945 the House of Hohenzollern was not restored with it. The ex-Crown Prince had frittered away his life on a succession of mistresses; in 1951 he died and was buried in the uniform of a Death's Head Hussar in the family vault at Hohen-zollernburg Castle near Hechingen. But significantly, although representatives of his own and other German royal houses attended the funeral, all wore civilian dress – a far cry from the long lost days of the Wilhelmine Empire. Appropriately one of the wreaths sent for the occasion bore the initial 'N' and a crown; it was sent by the Bonapartist pretender to the throne of France. The Hohenzollerns too had been finally reduced to the status of pre-tenders, tolerated as ordinary German citizens, but scarcely honoured, among the people whom once they had ruled with such flair and with so many grotesque errors.

6 (Above left) Wilhelm II, 'the Kaiser', with his son, Crown Prince Wilhelm.

7 (Above right) The Kaiser and his wife, Augusta Victoria of Schleswig-Holstein (Dona), with three of their grandchildren, the eldest children of the Crown Prince.

8 (Below) A snapshot of the liberal and progressive Crown Prince Frederick, tall and bearded, at a skating party. Later he was to rule for only 99 days before dying of cancer of the throat on 15 June 1888.

9 *Crown Prince Frederick with his wife Victoria, the eldest daughter of Queen Victoria of England, and their seven children. The future Kaiser is standing to the right of the picture; the future Queen Sophie of Greece is sitting with her hat on her lap.*

10 (Above left) Crown Prince Rudolph of Austria with the Kaiser (right) as a young man. Wilhelm's handicapped hand and arm are very noticeable in the picture.

11 (Below) The Palace gardens at Potsdam, one of the Kaiser's sixty palaces. Here the Empress is walking with the Crown Princess (in the white hat) and her three young sons.

12 (Above right) There was a strong Hohenzollern tradition that uniforms were the work-clothes of the family. Here Princess Alexandra Victoria of Prussia, wife of the

Kaiser's 4th son, August Wilhelm, wears the uniform of Colonel-in-Chief of the 14th Regiment of Dragoons.

13 (Above, opposite) Edward VII of England and Queen Alexandra on a visit to the Kaiser in 1909. Left to right: the Queen of Spain, Edward VII, Dona, the Kaiser, Queen Alexandra, the Queen of Portugal, Alfonso XIII of Spain, the Queen of Norway.

14 (Below, opposite) Two emperors: a picture taken before the First World War of the Kaiser and the Tsar travelling down the Kiel Canal in a launch.

15 (Above, opposite) At Trieste the Kaiser was photographed with Archduke Franz Ferdinand, heir to the Austrian Empire, whose assassination at Sarajevo was to spark off the First World War.

16 (Below, opposite) The Kaiser lecturing his generals on military manoeuvres just before the First World War.

17 (Above left) The Kaiser (centre) with Count Zeppelin on a visit to inspect one of the aviator's new dirigibles.

18 (Below left) A lover of blood sports, the Kaiser always dressed in style for sporting occasions.

19 (Above right) The Kaiser with his daughter, the Duchess of Brunswick, and his dogs, Hans and Erdmann – his favourite dachshund.

20 (Below right) Here Wilhelm is dressed as a huntsman, talking to his friend von Kessel. He took great delight in hunting and slaughtering animals, perhaps as proof that a withered arm was no deterrent to such activities.

21 (Above left) The Imperial Yacht at Kiel. The three little sons of the Crown Prince wore S.M.S. Hohenzollern caps. Left to right: the Duchess of Brunswick, the Crown Princess, Prince Hubertus, the Kaiser, the Crown Prince's eldest son (Prince Wilhelm), Prince Adalbert and Prince Louis Ferdinand.

22 (Below left) The Kaiser is pictured on the Imperial Yacht, the Hohenzollern, hiding Easter eggs. He much enjoyed practical jokes.

23 Bismarck, the 'Iron Chancellor' and the architect of modern Germany, whom Wilhelm II sacked in 1890.

24 The King of Italy on a visit to the Kaiser in 1911. Wilhelm called him 'the dwarf'.

25 (Above, opposite) The Kaiser dressed up as Frederick the Great, whom he liked to think he resembled, against a background of soldiers wearing uniforms of the period.

26 (Below left, opposite) Empress Augusta (Dona), a submissive and gentle character who before her marriage was a princess of Schleswig-Holstein. Bismarck referred to her as 'the cow from Holstein', but Wilhelm was deeply grieved by her death in 1921, when they were living in exile.

27 (Below right, opposite) Crown Prince Wilhelm ('Little Willie') with his wife on holiday in Heligoland after the First World War.

28 (Below left) The Central Powers: the Kaiser in the early days of the war, with his allies Emperor Franz Joseph of Austria (seated), Sultan Mehmet V of Turkey and Tsar Ferdinand of Bulgaria (standing, centre).

29 (Below right) A snapshot of Crown Prince Wilhelm (far right) with some of his officers during the First World War.

30 (Below) Wilhelm was fond of distributing mementoes. Here, he and his dachshund, Erdmann, give out medals and portraits of himself to the non-commissioned officers of the Potsdam garrison before the First World War.

31 *The bearded ex-Kaiser after the war, with his son, ex-Crown Prince Wilhelm (left) and the Crown Prince's eldest son, Prince Wilhelm, on the right.*

32 *Princess Cecilia of Prussia, the ex-Crown Prince's daughter, in a picture taken in Germany in 1938. She often visited her friend Lady Jellicoe in England.*

33 *(Below) Ex-Crown Prince Wilhelm returned to Germany in 1923; he soon acquired the reputation of a playboy, and the nickname of 'Little Willie'.*

34 *The Kaiser enjoyed a tranquil old age in exile, at Doorn in Holland. The picture shows him walking in Doorn with his second wife, Princess Hermine.*

35 *Ex-Crown Prince Wilhelm in the uniform of the Death's Head Hussars. On his death in 1951 he was buried wearing this uniform, in the family vault at Hohenzollernburg Castle.*

36 *Prince August Wilhelm of Prussia, the Kaiser's son, who with his brother Oscar joined the Nazi party in 1931.*

37 *Prince Wilhelm of Prussia, the eldest son of the ex-Crown Prince, with his wife, Dorothea von Salviati. He was later killed in action during the invasion of France fighting for the German army.*

38 *(Below) The Nazi Prince August Wilhelm attending a service in Paris in memory of the German war dead, in 1939.*

39 *(Above left, opposite) The ex-Kaiser's second wife, Princess Hermine.*

40 *(Below left, opposite) Prince August Wilhelm with his wife.*

41 *(Above right, opposite) The wife of the Nazi Prince August Wilhelm with one of their sons.*

42 *(Below right, opposite) The christening of the daughter of Prince and Princess Frederick of Prussia, which took place in Surrey in 1952. The Duchess of Kent (holding the baby) was a godmother.*

Chapter Two

The Hapsburgs

As the twentieth century began, the venerable and illustrious House of Hapsburg held sway over the ill-assorted Austro-Hungarian Empire. In contrast, the Hohenzollerns and the House of Saxe-Coburg-Gotha, to which Queen Victoria belonged, by marriage, were crude upstarts, for the Hapsburgs had ruled a great empire when Germany had been a fragmented and disorderly array of principalities, and when the Tudors had scarcely established themselves upon the English throne.

At the centre of the Austrian imperial system in 1900 was Franz Joseph, Emperor since 1848. He was no longer an absolute monarch, and his royal prerogative was circumscribed by constitutional limitations. None the less he was the one fixed star in the imperial firmament; governments could rise and fall, parliamentary factions could quarrel and reunite, the subject races of the empire could strain at the bonds which held them, but Franz Joseph lent a stability to the system simply by being there and, apparently, hardly changing his attitudes throughout.

He was, intrinsically, a blinkered, humourless and conservative man. He lived a curiously isolated life, not mixing much with the aristocracy but confining his social contacts almost exclusively to members of his own Imperial House, who included sixty-five archdukes and archduchesses. Even when he attended some great social occasion like the Court Ball, which was restricted to the diplomatic corps, army officers on active service in Vienna, the aristocracy and the royal family, he saw his chief duty as representing the majesty of the sovereign.

Franz Joseph viewed his constitutional function, according to a contemporary biographer, as that of 'a kind of civil servant without initiative and without prominence. He accepted it simply, sadly, as a duty and a discipline.' The traumatic events of the year of his accession, the great European revolutions of 1848, had shaken his throne and had forced him to abandon the policy-making role of his predecessors. So he worked on like a frugal, punctual civil servant, steadily signing the state papers put before him. He began his paper work at 5 a.m. and carried on through lunchtime, sustained at his desk by a quickly taken meal. He read few of these documents in detail, though each day he scanned the press cuttings, seeking to understand public opinion. Since he took his role as a constitutional monarch so seriously, he seemed to take on the colour of whatever government was in office and merely to reflect opinions which predominated in his realm.

His one relaxation was hunting. But here again it was not the flamboyant, and occasionally grotesque, hunting habits of the Kaiser Wilhelm II that he favoured. Franz Joseph preferred to stalk stag and chamois in the mountains, to lie patiently in wait for black-cock and wood-grouse. He enjoyed the solitary hunt, which called into play his stealth and skill. He was a good hunter and boasted of his prowess in his private correspondence, but his chosen sport was as discreet and unremarkable as his exercise of Imperial power.

Franz Joseph's personal life was an unpleasant combination of isolation and terrible family tragedy. His Empress, the beautiful and still youthful Elizabeth, had found him a limited and unresponsive partner. Though he continued to love and admire her as an example of perfect womanhood, she stayed away from her husband, the Imperial court, even Austria, for months each year. The Empress went on Mediterranean holidays, rode to hounds in England, or visited Hungary, where she enjoyed a remarkable popularity. She had been further alienated from her husband by the latter's excessive dependence on his mother, the autocratic and domineering Archduchess Sophie.

In compensation for her marital unhappiness the Empress Elizabeth had focused her attentions upon her eldest son, the Crown Prince Rudolph. Whereas the Emperor was sober and restrained, well-tutored, though without much intellectual curiosity, the Crown Prince was clever, rash and pleasure-loving. He travelled widely and wrote two books about his journeys; he sought friends and public approval; he mixed freely with Viennese intellectuals and became the darling of progressives and democrats throughout the Empire. His private life was less inspiring: despite his marriage to a Belgian princess, Stephanie, he continued to consort with women from high society and from the demi-monde, and two years before his death in 1889 he was treated for an illness which was, in all probability, syphilis.

Rudolph committed suicide in January 1889. The exact reasons for this act are difficult to define, and the archives do not yield conclusive evidence. There is no doubt that he did not see eye to eye with his father on the future role of the Imperial monarchy, and he seemed to be getting into deep water through his Hungarian sympathies. He was also actively contemplating divorce, an unthinkable step for the heir to the House of Hapsburg. More intriguing was his relationship with his young mistress, the naïve and pretty Marie von Vetsera, who had died with him at the hunting lodge of Mayerling in the Wienerwald. Certainly Rudolph had talked a good deal of suicide and death-pacts to other mistresses; he was also known to be heavily in debt. (Another story that circulated after his death was that a jealous game-keeper had castrated him, and that he had then killed himself in despair!)

At any rate, what is certain is that Rudolph and Marie von Vetsera both died in tragic circumstances at Mayerling. With the Crown Prince perished the vague and over-optimistic hopes of the Viennese middle class that somehow he would supervise a new enlightened epoch of Hapsburg rule. The Archduke Franz Ferdinand, the Emperor's nephew, now became heir presumptive and was, ironically, to be the victim of the fateful assassination at Sarajevo in 1914. The new heir was, however, by no means as popular as the dead Rudolph, and the feeling gained ground that the Hapsburg monarchy would not survive the Emperor's death.

Franz Joseph found some comfort in the bleak later years of his reign in the company of a popular young actress Katharina Schratt. The Empress Elizabeth had engineered their first meeting, and Franz Joseph fell deeply in love with this attractive, lively and buxom young woman. Katharina Schratt supplied tit-bits of theatre gossip, fed him well, provided appropriate company for him, and even managed to fit in with his spartan time-table – he would often call on her at seven o'clock in the morning. For his part, he allowed her to pursue her professional life and even interfered (though ineffectually) in a dispute she was having with the new director of the Burgtheater.

The Empress Elizabeth went out of her way to befriend Katharina Schratt, who was, after all, helping to dispel the Emperor's loneliness. She made her friendship with the actress known to the public, while, more privately, the two women dieted together. Of course it is arguable that the Empress's motives were more selfish than they appeared: by openly acknowledging Katharina Schratt's place in her husband's affections she probably helped to ensure that Franz Joseph would never overthrow her completely – indeed it was claimed that Katharina never became his mistress in the technical sense. That the Empress's attitude was a complex one can be assumed from the malicious verses that she composed:

> Imbued with aping mania,
>   Despite her pounds of fat,
> She longs to play Titania . . .
>   That Katharina Schratt.

In September 1898 the Empress herself was assassinated in the most dramatic circumstances. An anarchist of Italian parentage, Luigi Luccheni, had vowed to kill the first royal person that he encountered. Having failed to encounter the Duc d'Orléans, a descendant of Louis Philippe, Luccheni travelled to Geneva and there plunged a sharpened file into the breast of the Empress as she prepared to board a steamer on Lake Léman. Luccheni was sentenced to life imprisonment but later hanged himself in jail. For Franz Joseph the blow was a terrible one, and he justifiably complained that 'Nothing has been spared me in this world'. The dead Empress was brought back to lie in state in the Imperial Chapel of the Hofburg, and was later buried in the Hapsburg vault between her dead son Rudolph and her brother-in-law, the executed Maximilian, Emperor of Mexico.

As Elizabeth's devoted Hungarian subjects prepared to build a monument near her tomb, unsavoury scandal lapped round the Imperial family. A Countess Larische, who was a niece of the dead Empress and who knew a great deal about the private lives of her aunt and of the late Crown Prince Rudolph, threatened to reveal the intimate secrets of the House of Hapsburg to the world's press. Franz Joseph had no choice but to buy her off. Apparently his first offer consisted of 2,500 dollars and a castle in a remote corner of the Empire, but, wisely fearing imprisonment in the castle, Countess Larische settled for voluntary exile in the United States and 25,000 dollars.

In the years before the outbreak of the First World War the Archduke Franz Ferdinand became the most powerful and the most feared man in the Empire. He owed his callous and despotic streak to his grandfather, the notorious King Bomba of Naples; he hardly ever smiled in public and was noted for his cold staring eyes and his pompous strut. He collected antiques and tended his rose gardens, but above all he revelled in the hunt: he was a deadly shot and in his lifetime slaughtered hundreds of thousands of birds and animals. Once, when shooting with the Kaiser Wilhelm II, sixty boars were driven before his guns; he bagged fifty-nine of them but was incensed that one wounded creature escaped him. He was, in fact, an exterminator of wild animals rather than a huntsman. After a day's shooting, the Archduke and his guests would return to the hunting lodge, bathe in wooden wash-tubs before a blazing fire of pine logs and then eat a hearty dinner. A typical dinner would consist of clear soup, freshly caught trout, a saddle of roebuck garnished with sauce, and an open jam tart. From the walls the trophied heads of chamois, roebuck and red deer gazed down while the royal party drank Viennese beer, sweet champagne and Hungarian wine.

One of the few redeeming features of Franz Ferdinand's character was his passionate devotion to his Czech wife, the Countess Sophie Chotek. The Hapsburgs considered the once-destitute Sophie to be an upstart, and she suffered countless indignities at their hands. She was excluded from the most intimate functions of the court; she could not sit at her own dining table if royalty were present; she could not appear with her husband in the royal box at the Opera, whereas her sister-in-law the Archduchess Maria Annunziata, now first Lady of the Empire, could.

Franz Ferdinand also clashed with his uncle Franz Joseph over the future development of the Empire. The former wanted to replace the failing Dual Monarchy of Austria and Hungary with a closely controlled federal system which would grant some degree of autonomy to the ten main ethnic groups living within the Empire. In this way Franz Ferdinand hoped to solve the Southern Slav question by reconciling Serbia to a looser Imperial control. The old Emperor, however, thought little of these federalist plans and was sympathetic to those who argued that it would be necessary to crush the inconvenient independence of Serbia in order to pacify the Southern Slavs.

In the summer of 1914 there was no indication of impending doom. In Vienna, *Elektra* was playing at the Opera, and the Nijinskys saw the performance; to the south, Franz Ferdinand was attending army manoeuvres in Bosnia under a scorching sun. On 28 June the Archduke and his wife paid an official visit to Sarajevo, a town some fifty miles from the Serbian frontier. 28 June was St Vitus's Day, a day of reckoning in the calendar of the Southern Slavs – the anniversary of the Battle of Kossovo where five hundred years earlier the Turks had conquered the Serbs, and also a day of celebration for the Serbian triumph in the 1912 war against the Turks. In this hostile environment the Archduke and his wife were shot dead by Gavrilo Princip, a Serbian student and member of a secret nationalist movement 'Young Bosnia'.

The old Emperor heard the news of yet another family catastrophe as he sat, his head bowed in despair, in the Schönbrunn palace. Finally he declared, 'Horrible, horrible. One cannot play tricks with the Almighty. A Higher Power has restored the order that I myself was unable to maintain.' This was a clear reference to the Crown Prince Rudolph's suicide, but also to the fact that the new heir to the throne was the popular young Archduke Karl, Franz Joseph's great-nephew.

The funeral arrangements for the assassinated Archduke and his wife provided a bizarre illustration of the stultifying protocol surrounding the House of Hapsburg. The family considered it unthinkable that Sophie Chotek should lie in the Imperial vault, so it was claimed that the late Archduke had wished to be buried in the chapel of his castle at Art-stetten on the Danube. In the brief funeral mass held in the Royal Chapel of the Hofburg and attended by Franz Joseph, other members of the Imperial family were conspicuously absent; moreover, Sophie's coffin was placed at a lower level than her husband's to indicate her lower rank; the only wreath from the Imperial family came from the widow of the Crown Prince Rudolph, though the dead couple's children brought flowers. At last the coffins were borne to their final resting place amid a violent thunderstorm and along flooded paths, and later the public learnt with horror that on the funeral ferry-boat the

44 Empress Elizabeth of Austria, the beautiful wife of Franz Joseph. Unhappy with her husband, she spent much of her time travelling abroad; for his part he never ceased to love her.

coffin of the Archduke had almost been allowed to plunge into the waters of the Danube.

A great clamour arose in the Austrian press and was expressed at public meetings and in the highest military circles: Serbia must be made to pay for the outrage of the Archduke's assassination – for few doubted that behind Princip and his fellow conspirators stood the Serbian authorities. On 23 July Austria-Hungary delivered a humiliating ultimatum to Serbia, the acceptance of which would have clearly been inconsistent with the Slav state's independence. Serbia did accept the terms of the ultimatum, though with some reservations, but the Austrian warlords found the response inadequate. During the last days of June the crowned heads of Europe bombarded each other with telegrams, hoping to avoid a general war. On 28 July Franz Joseph, at eighty-four the oldest crowned head of them all, sat at his desk at his villa at Bad Ischl and signed the declaration of war. Though those who wanted war believed that Austria now had a chance to smash the insolent Serbs once and for all, the old Emperor was, in fact, sealing the fate not only of his own ancient dynasty but also of other European royal houses.

But the war did not provide Austria-Hungary with the military success that was needed to keep the Empire together. Though the stubborn Serbs were conquered by November 1914, on the eastern front the Russians were pushing over the Carpathians, while, after 1915, the Italians were making progress in the Tyrolean Alps. Cosmopolitan, sophisticated Vienna was starved of good music, almost every able-bodied man was called up, and in the famous coffee houses the customers drank a brew made mostly from chicory which they sweetened with saccharine.

As if to symbolize the gloomy times, the eighty-six-year-old Emperor died in November 1916, having reigned longer than any contemporary monarch – including Queen Victoria. Franz Joseph suffered an attack of bronchitis and took to his bed on 22 November, telling his valet to call him at 3.30 a.m. since he was behind with his work. At 9 p.m. that same day he woke in a fit of coughing, gulped down some tea, and died as tidily as he had reigned.

Amid widespread grief the old Emperor's body was transferred to the Hofburg Chapel to lie in state for a week. Thousands filed by to pay their respects: the war-wounded hobbling by, the pious, the curious, and those respectful elderly citizens who saw in Franz Joseph's death the inevitable death of the monarchy itself. The mourners found the coffin closed, for the corpse had become unpresentably disfigured during the embalming process. On 31 November 1916 the funeral procession made its way through crowded streets to the Imperial vault at the Capuchin monastery; the street lamps were shrouded in black crêpe as, with muffled drums, the units of foot soldiers and cavalry passed by.

At the doors of the Imperial vault the coffin was set down, and the Hapsburg's Master of Ceremonies knocked three times with his mace. The Father Guardian called out, from behind the doors, 'Who demands entrance?' 'His Apostolic Majesty, the Emperor,' came the reply. 'I know him not,' answered the monk. Again three knocks. 'Who demands entry here?' 'The all-high sovereign, the Emperor Franz.' 'I know him not.' For a third time the Master of Ceremonies knocked at the doors. 'In the name of God, who wishes to enter?' 'Your brother Franz, a poor sinner.' At this, the doors were opened and Franz Joseph's coffin went to lie between those of his assassinated wife and his suicide son.

The young archduke now became the Emperor Karl I, the last of the Hapsburgs. Although the 1917 revolutions in Russia eventually removed that adversary from Austria's eastern front, the Italian campaign was proving extremely costly and, in any case, the entry of the

United States into the war in April more than offset the loss of Russia on the Allied side. The German High Command did little to hide their view that the Austrian Empire was an inferior ally and, indeed, a burden. The prospect of the premature collapse of the Empire caused Karl to sue for a separate peace at the behest of his advisers. The new Emperor's brother-in-law, Prince Sixtus, actually went on a peace mission to President Poincaré of France, but neither Italy nor Germany would allow a separate Austrian peace settlement.

So the Austro-Hungarian Empire, its subject races straining to break away from central authority, was dragged down to ruin with Imperial Germany and Turkey. By October 1918 the Allies had pushed the German armies out of Flanders; Austrian forces had been ejected from the Balkans and had suffered a crushing defeat at Italian hands at Vittorio Veneto; Turkey was on the point of collapse. On 28 October the Emperor reluctantly agreed to recognize the independence of Czechoslovakia and Yugoslavia; he also renounced the German alliance, and his government began to negotiate peace terms. On 3 November Austria signed an armistice with Italy, and on the next day an armistice with Britain and France.

The war had been lost, at the cost of four million casualties and the destruction of the Empire. Revolutionary crowds surged through Vienna and other cities calling for a republic and socialism. At the Schönbrunn palace the Emperor and his Empress, Zita, waited as disaster upon disaster was announced. Their royal guard melted away, and in the end only the cadets of the Wiener Neustadt Military Academy could be relied upon to protect them.

On 9 November the Emperor was presented with a document of abdication. He had no choice but to sign it, and in the blue Chinese room the Hapsburg monarchy ended with a signature. Next morning, Sunday, the Emperor made his last public appearance at the Schönbrunn chapel, and for the last time the organ played *Gott Erhalte Unsern Kaiser* ('God Preserve our Emperor'). The next evening two cars drew up at the Schönbrunn, and the socialist leader Karl Renner announced, 'Herr Hapsburg, the taxi is waiting.'

The Hapsburgs were carried off to Switzerland and exile; on 12 November the black and yellow Imperial flag was hauled down and the red and white flags of the republic fluttered over a destitute and starving Vienna. The peace treaties hacked the Austrian Empire to fragments; Austria itself was left as one-eighth of the original whole, with under seven million inhabitants of whom two million lived in Vienna, once the great Imperial heart but now without its body and limbs.

But all was not lost for the Hapsburgs. In 1920 the National Assembly in Budapest restored the monarchist constitution and named Admiral Horthy as Regent for the departed Karl. In March 1921 the ex-Emperor was smuggled over the Swiss frontier disguised as a gardener; he travelled third-class to Vienna and was then taken into Hungary. Here his hopes were crushed, for Admiral Horthy refused to hand over power to him and he had to beat an undignified retreat.

In October 1921 Karl attempted a coup d'état. He and his wife landed by plane at Sopron in Hungary, where he called upon the local garrison to support him, and even set up a cabinet. The government ordered him to leave the country, but he defied them and led a march against Budapest. Though there were government fears that many Hungarian officers would be disloyal to the Regent, the royalist forces were routed shortly after Karl's train drew in at Bicske railway station. Karl and his wife were confined at Count Esterhazy's castle at Tata, where a mob broke in and were narrowly prevented from assassinating the royal couple. They were then interned in the monastery at Tihany, and a final statement of abdication was forced out of Karl. At last they were shipped aboard H.M.S. *Glow-worm* on the Danube and eventually transported to Madeira by the good offices of the British government.

Four months after arriving in Madeira, Karl died of tuberculosis. But still the Hapsburg cause was not dead. In July 1923 Vienna saw a demonstration in memory of the dead ex-Emperor; the demonstration became disorderly and a good many arrests were made. Even later, as conflict deepened between the Socialist and the right-wing Christian Socialist parties in Austria, the Heimwehr – the armed branch of the latter party – contemplated a coup that would restore the young Archduke Otto von Hapsburg to the throne of Austria. But the Heimwehr's attempted *Putsch* in 1929 failed, and the Hapsburgs saw instead the rise of Hitler to supreme authority over Austria as a result of the *Anschluss* of 1938.

Otto von Hapsburg, the pretender to the throne of his ancestors, went to live in Belgium in the castle of Steenockerzeel with his widowed mother. He took a degree at the University of Louvain. He later moved to Bavaria, taking up residence in a large country house near Pöcking, where he still lives. He developed a keen interest in sociology and political science, and wrote and lectured on these subjects. In 1960 he gave lectures in London and Cambridge on the subject of 'Monarchy in the Atomic Age'; it was a symbolic adaptation to changed and straitened circumstances, and old Franz Joseph must have stirred uneasily in his tomb.

45 Baroness Marie von Vetsera, the mistress of Crown Prince Rudolph, the heir to the throne. Marie died with Rudolph in a suicide pact in 1889 at Mayerling. This portrait of her was found in a locket on Rudolph's body at his death.

46 Princess Stephanie of Belgium, Rudolph's wife. She was the daughter of Leopold of Belgium and a favourite niece of Queen Victoria. She was only sixteen when she married Rudolph, who took his mistress with him when he went to Brussels for his wedding.

47 A typically dashing portrait of Crown Prince Rudolph.

46

48 (Above, opposite) Franz Joseph's family included sixty-five archdukes and archduchesses. In this group Archduke Karl Ludwig stands on the left, Emperor Franz Joseph sits stiffly on the sofa; behind him is his brother, the ill-fated Emperor Maximilian of Mexico, who was executed by his subjects. The other is Archduke Ludwig-Victor.

49 (Below left, opposite) The lovely Empress Elizabeth, assassinated by an anarchist at Geneva in September 1898.

50 (Below right, opposite) Franz Joseph deep in prayer (or thought) in 1914. In July the 84-year-old Emperor signed the declaration of war on Serbia which plunged Europe into the First World War.

51-52 Archduke Franz Ferdinand, Franz Joseph's unattractive and unpopular nephew, became his heir on the suicide of Crown Prince Rudolph. Two family groups with his wife, the Czech Countess Sophie Chotek, who was despised as an upstart by the other Hapsburgs, and their children.

53 (Above, opposite) Emperor Franz Joseph playing host to the crafty and successful King Carol of Romania and his poetess wife, Queen Elizabeth (seated), who wrote under the name of Carmen Sylva.

54 (Below left, opposite) Franz Joseph's great relaxation was hunting. He loved to hunt alone, stalking stag or shooting black-cock.

55 (Below right, opposite) This sentimental, patriotic photograph was taken on Franz Joseph's birthday.

56 (Above left) In 1907, at the age of seventy-seven, Franz Joseph rode out to the military manoeuvres.

57 (Below left) Imperial Vienna in 1913. The aged Emperor can be seen in the centre of the picture, surrounded by a colourful procession.

58 Archduke Franz Ferdinand at the military manoeuvres of 1914, in Bosnia. A few days later, he and his wife were shot dead at Sarajevo.

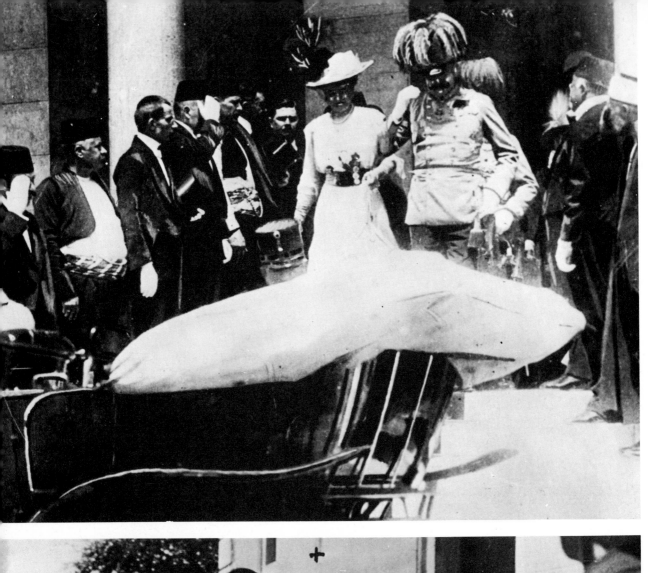

59 (Above, opposite) The assassination at Sarajevo, 28 June 1914. Seconds after this photograph of Franz Ferdinand and Sophie was taken, the shots which killed them were fired.

60 (Below, opposite) The arrest of Gavrilo Princip, the fanatic Serbian student who was the assassin at Sarajevo. Few Austrians doubted that the Serbian authorities were behind the assassin and his fellow conspirators.

61 Franz Ferdinand and Sophie lying in the Royal Chapel of the Hofburg, Vienna. They were buried at Artstetten to avoid the necessity of burying the despised Sophie in the Imperial Vault.

62 Zita, the wife of the new heir to the Austrian throne, Franz Joseph's great-nephew, the young and popular Archduke Karl.

63 Archduke Karl succeeded to the throne on Franz Joseph's death in November 1916, becoming Emperor Karl I, the last Emperor of Austria.

64 (Below) Karl (front, second from the left) during the War, with Prince Leopold of Bavaria (centre) and General Woyrsch.

65 (Right) Karl's coronation portrait. Despite the Crown of St Stephen and the Hungarian coronation robes, he was to reign for only two years.

66 (Left) Karl I and Empress Zita. Karl was forced to abdicate on 9 November 1918. He left the Schonbrunn Palace as 'Herr Hapsburg'. After an abortive bid for power in Hungary in 1921, he died of tuberculosis a year later.

67 Karl's eldest son, Archduke Otto, taking his brothers and sisters for a drive on a Spanish beach in a car which was a sixteenth-birthday present from King Alfonso of Spain.

68 Karl and Zita on the Bosphorus in 1918, on a visit to Constantinople.

69 *Wilhelmina Adamovitch, an actress from a peasant family in the Carpathians, married Archduke Leopold Ferdinand in 1903; they were divorced in 1907 and she eventually died in poverty.*

70 *Archduke Albrecht of Austria, whose claims to the Hungarian throne were thought by many to have some hope of success, renounced all his claims on his morganatic marriage at Brighton to a divorcée.*

71 *Leopold Ferdinand in 1908 with his second wife, the equally plebeian Fraulein Maria Ritter.*

72 *Archduke Robert of Austria came to London after Hitler's Anschluss of 1938 as a spokesman for a free Austria, liberated from Hitler's rule.*

73 *(Right) Archduke Eugene of Hapsburg (centre) taking part in the Corpus Christi procession in Vienna in 1934, the first member of the Imperial family to make a public appearance in Vienna since Karl I's abdication in 1918.*

74 *(Below right) Archduke Eugene (left) being received by the Austrian Chancellor, Dollfuss, on his return from exile in 1934. Eugene's enthusiastic reception from the crowds, however, did not lead to any change of fortune for the Hapsburgs.*

75 *(Left) Barred from rule, some Hapsburgs succeeded in other fields. Princess Margit of Austria (here apparently interrogating her doll) was pronounced, by an international jury at an exhibition held by a child welfare organization in Budapest, to be the biggest and best developed child of her age in Hungary.*

76 *Archduke Otto, Karl I's heir, standing on the border between Austria and Germany. It was not until 1966 that he was granted a passport which enabled him to enter Austria, which he had left in 1918 with his mother, Empress Zita, when he was only seven years old.*

77 Archduke Franz Joseph of Austria living in a very different style from his namesake, the Emperor Franz Joseph, dancing with his wife Marie at a ball at the Waldorf Astoria Hotel in New York.

78 The Hapsburgs' only link with their former glory is in their appearances at royal occasions. Here Archduchess Elizabeth of Austria (second from left standing next to Princess Anne) is a bridesmaid at the wedding of Princess Alexandra to Mr Angus Ogilvy at Westminster Abbey, 1963.

79 (Below) Archduke Otto, trying to put his Volkswagen in order on one of his European lecture tours.

80 (Right) Archduke Otto with his family at their home, Pocking, in Bavaria. His wife, Regina, holds the baby Walburga. The other four girls are, from left to right, Gabriela, Andrea, Monika and Michaela.

Chapter Three

The Ruin of the Romanovs

Tsar Nicholas II ascended to the Russian throne in 1894, succeeding his father, the physically imposing and autocratic Alexander III. In contrast, Nicholas was slight of stature and modest and hesitant in nature, though indubitably conscientious and anxious to serve his country. But whereas Alexander's reign had been the last fling of unbridled autocracy, Nicholas was destined to see the monarchy's power clipped and finally destroyed completely; when Alexander died the Romanovs were firmly in the saddle of Imperial Russia, but his son and his family were to be murdered by the Bolsheviks in 1918.

Nicholas was born in 1864 and appears to have enjoyed a secure and happy childhood. He had two brothers, George and Michael, and two sisters, Xenia and Olga. They were brought up in the Anichkov Palace in St Petersburg, with a Scandinavian governess and a regime that included six o'clock awakenings and camp beds. In the summer they went to the Livadiya Palace on the Black Sea, where a great marble staircase led down to the shore. Nicholas's childhood provided him, however, with a terrible reminder of the danger that was never far from his family, for in 1881 he saw the mangled corpse of his assassinated grandfather Alexander II lying in the Winter Palace in St Petersburg.

Alexander III had placed his eldest son's education in the hands of the ultra-conservative General Gregory Danilovich, who inculcated into his charge the stoic virtues of self-discipline, reserve and a blind faith in God and Tsar. There was also an English tutor, Charles Heath, who taught Nicholas to speak and write excellent English. French was also taught to the royal children, and one instructor marvelled at 'the docility, gentleness and submissiveness of the grand-dukes. . . . I have never caught a bit of boredom, lassitude, or impatience.' Perhaps this submissiveness reflected the lack of an enquiring intellect or of a vivid imagination. Certainly Nicholas seems to have emerged from his formal education with a dull and rather closed mind.

Of the Tsarevich's simple good nature and generosity there is no lack of evidence. His cousin, the future King George V, to whom he bore an almost incredibly close resemblance, was extremely fond of him and told Queen Victoria in 1894 that 'Nicky has been kindness itself to me, he is the same dear boy he has always been to me & talks to me quite openly on every subject'. When he became an officer in the Hussars at the age of eighteen his conscientious and good-natured conduct made him popular with his fellow-officers. Nicholas greatly enjoyed his career as an army officer, revelling in the comradeship and the limited responsibility of his new life.

Self-effacing and not particularly clever, Nicholas was much in awe of his father and kept so much in the background at court functions that one observer wrote, 'He so much loses himself in the crowd that it is difficult to distinguish him from the mass. A little Hussar officer, not ill-favoured, but commonplace, insignificant.' When Witte, Minister for

81 The Russian court was noted for its splendour. Here the Tsar and Tsarina are shown wearing Russian Imperial costumes of the Middle Ages.

Communications, proposed that he should be president of a committee concerned with the construction of the Trans-Siberia Railway, Alexander III expostulated, 'But do you know the Grand Duke, my heir? Have you ever had a serious conversation with him? He is a child. His reasoning is childish. How could he preside over this committee?' None the less Nicholas got the job and acquitted himself well enough.

In the early 1890s it seemed appropriate to consider a bride for Nicholas, who had already installed his mistress, the ballerina Matilda Kshessinska, in a St Petersburg mansion. Among the prospective brides was the Kaiser's youngest sister Princess Margaret and a French princess of the fallen house of Bourbon. But Nicholas had already made his choice and was to insist upon it in one of his few examples of strong-mindedness.

His chosen bride, and the last Tsarina of Russia, was Princess Alix of Hesse-Darmstadt, who numbered among her ancestors Mary Queen of Scots and St Elizabeth of Thuringia. Alix's mother, the fourth daughter of Queen Victoria, had died when the little girl was six; subsequently Alix had been brought up in England under the watchful but not unkindly eye of Queen Victoria. She was now a strikingly beautiful young woman, golden-haired and blue-eyed, though reserved and deeply religious. Nicholas pressed his claims in the summer of 1894 while attending the wedding celebrations of the Grand Duke of Hesse at Coburg. He recorded that 'She looked particularly pretty but extremely sad. They left us alone, and then began between us that talk I so long wanted and so much feared. We talked to twelve but with no result; she still objects to changing her religion. Poor girl, she cried a lot.'

But within a few days Alix had agreed to embrace the Orthodox faith, and a few weeks later the betrothed couple were holidaying as guests of their mutual grandmother Queen Victoria. In the autumn of 1894, however, Alexander III was told that he was dying. Alix was hastily summoned to the Crimea to receive his blessing. She had also summed up her prospective husband's lack of drive and self-assertiveness and urged him:

Sweet child, pray to God . . . Your Sunny is praying for you and the beloved patient . . . Be firm and make the doctors . . . come alone to you every day . . . so that you are always the first to know. Don't let others be put first and you left out . . . Show your own mind and don't let others forget who you are.

While in the Crimea, Alix made her conversion to the Orthodox religion and was re-named Alexandra Fedorovna. In November 1894, after the death of Alexander III, the new Tsar and she were married in the chapel of the Winter Palace; Nicholas wore his red Hussar's uniform with a white cloak over one shoulder, while Alexandra's gown was made of dazzling white silk, with a gold brocade mantle. There was little doubt that the new Tsar and the Tsarina were devotedly in love, and Nicholas noted in his diary that his was 'the greatest bliss on this earth', while Alexandra wrote, 'I would never have believed that one could have so perfect a happiness in this world, such a sentiment of unity between two human beings.'

The early years of Nicholas's reign, however, were hardly blissful. The young Tsar leant heavily on his mother for advice (to the annoyance of his wife) and deferred too readily to his formidable and quarrelsome Romanov uncles and cousins. At his coronation in May 1896, the Order of St Andrew, one of the most venerable and august decorations of the

82 *A Russian royal family group. Tsar Alexander III (Nicholas's father) is seated. During Alexander III's lifetime, no one doubted that the Romanovs were firmly in the saddle.*

83 *(Below left) Grand Duke Boris Vladimirovich (right) with another prince, relaxing with a Viennese actress at Ostend just before the First World War.*

84 *Grand Duke Nicholas Nicholaevich, the Tsar's able and popular cousin. He was appointed Commander-in-Chief of the Russian forces on the outbreak of war in 1914; the Tsar became Commander-in-Chief himself in Grand Duke Nicholas's place in 1915.*

Empire, fell from his shoulders in a portentous clatter, and later at Khodinka hundreds of the Tsar's humbler subjects lost their lives in an unseemly tumult as they waited to receive the new sovereign's bounty in the form of food, drink and mementoes.

Nicholas was singularly ill-suited to head off the demands for a greater participation by the people in affairs of state. Ambassadors and foreign dignitaries combined to sing the praises of his good manners and unpretentious bearing, but in fact he was a ruler of sadly limited abilities. Though reasonably intelligent he was quite incapable of making the best use of advice and personal experience; he chose his ministers without much insight and seemed to display little confidence in most of them; he abhorred uncomfortable scenes and unpleasant choices, and often remained impassive and silent in the face of bad news; foreign diplomats were also convinced that the Tsar tended to agree with whoever spoke to him last.

This was all a far cry from the heavy-handed certainties of Alexander III, yet, in his own way, Nicholas was just as autocratic. He revelled in the strength of the Russian army and in its great ceremonial parades which symbolically underwrote his regime. He also believed whole-heartedly that he had the sacred duty of maintaining unimpaired the autocratic structure bequeathed him by his father, and that if he shared power with the people they would proceed to 'efface the superior classes of society from the surface of the earth'.

Nicholas was increasingly supported in these views by his wife. Alexandra was inhibited and sullen in public, and she became an authoritarian figure within her immediate family. She also came to believe passionately in Russian autocracy, particularly cherishing the supposedly mystical union between the Tsar and the peasantry, and telling Queen Victoria that 'Russia is not England. Here it is not necessary to make efforts to gain popular affection.'

Unfortunately for the Romanovs, the autocratic convictions of the Tsar and Tsarina were manifestly unsuited to the early twentieth century. Russia was being transformed by a belated industrial revolution and by the growth of radical political activity. In 1898 the Russian Social Democratic party was founded and in 1903 split into a right-wing faction (the Mensheviks) and a left-wing faction (the Bolsheviks). The regime ruthlessly suppressed those whom it considered to be subversive, and Nicholas failed to comprehend the sincerity and strength of views of such subversives, and in particular their appeal to the new Russian proletariat.

Amid unofficial strikes, attempted assassinations and the unforgivable horrors of the anti-Jewish pogroms, Russia went to war with the rising power of Japan. The Russo-Japanese War of 1904–5 was fought in Manchuria, Korea and Far Eastern waters; both on land and at sea Russian forces suffered abrupt and humiliating defeats. In the unrest that attended these disasters can be seen the portents of the revolutions of 1917. The disturbances of 1905 were significant enough: in January hundreds of demonstrating, though not dis-loyal, workers were shot down in the square outside the Winter Palace in St Petersburg; in February Nicholas's uncle the Grand Duke Sergius was blown to pieces by an assassin's bomb in Moscow; in June a serious mutiny broke out on the *Potemkin*, a battleship in the Black Sea fleet; in October, after the ending of the war with Japan, there was a paralysing general strike and widespread agrarian unrest, and a worker's Soviet was established in St Petersburg. On 30 October the Tsar chose conciliation rather than repression and granted constitutional reform, including a Prime Minister (Witte), a legislature (the Duma) and some civil rights. The 'October Manifesto' split the revolutionaries, but a substantial number could not be bought off and fighting in Moscow and parts of the countryside persisted into 1906. An uneasy compromise ensued: the Tsar had tempered his autocratic rule, but hundreds of thousands of his subjects were unsatisfied by the reforms of 1905.

Throughout these tribulations the Tsar and his young family remained an intimate, closely-knit group. There were four daughters, Olga, Tatiana, Maria and Anastasia; in 1904, at last, a male heir was born, the Tsarevich Alexis. Devoted to one another, the family was perhaps never so happy as when staying at its main residence, the small Alexander Palace at Tsarskoe Selo some miles outside St Petersburg. By no means as grandiose as the Winter Palace (only briefly tenanted each year), nor as sumptuous as the royal hunting lodge at Spala in Poland, nor as impressive as the Black Sea palace at Livadiya, the Alexander Palace under the Tsarina's influence came to look like an English country mansion, despite the quartet of colourfully dressed Negro guards. The family's tastes were essentially simple, their games and pastimes unremarkable, their artistic interests fundamentally philistine, their conversation naïve and straightforward.

Yet the birth of the Tsarevich brought them great pain as well as great joy, for within six weeks of his birth he was found to be suffering from haemophilia. This disease, transmitted through female genes, was a crippling and potentially lethal disability. Due to the failure of the victim's blood to clot properly the smallest bruise could lead to the formation of swollen blood sacs, and a nose-bleed could mean death. The victim's joints also became paralysed through the internal accumulation of blood.

The royal family had to watch hawklike over the health of the unfortunate Tsarevich. His mother assumed the guilt for his condition, tortured herself with doubts and developed a variety of psychosomatic ailments. From 1906 the distraught Tsarina came to rely more and more upon the capacity of a disreputable monk, Rasputin, to tide the Tsarevich over his many crises. Rasputin's power to heal Alexis was probably an exercise in faith-healing; whether or not this was so, it gave him an especially privileged place in Russian society. The Tsarina Alexandra would hear nothing against him and refused to believe the numerous and authentic stories of his sexual excesses and his overbearing insolence. Since the Tsarevich's illness was kept a secret from the Russian people Rasputin's hold over the royal family seemed both inexplicable and bizarre. Moreover, Rasputin, naturally enough, bolstered the Tsar and Tsarina's belief in autocracy with homely theology and peasant-like homilies. There is no doubt that he supported Alexandra's convictions on this score and that she in turn supported the Tsar.

In addition to the Tsar's immediate family there were some sixty other Romanovs. They were a quarrelsome, charming, self-willed and occasionally talented breed. Nicholas's two sisters, the Grand Duchess Xenia and the Grand Duchess Olga, both married but with strikingly different results, for Xenia produced six sons and one daughter whereas Olga remained childless and instead became the most devoted aunt of the Tsar's children. Nicholas's younger brother George, reputed to be brilliant, died of tuberculosis in 1899. His youngest brother the Grand Duke Michael was renowned for his frank good humour, but in 1906 he sacrificed any influence he might have enjoyed over the Tsar by announcing his intention of marrying a twice-divorced commoner, Natalia. Michael was subsequently obliged to live abroad with his mistress, who bore him a son; in 1912 he horrified the Tsar and Tsarina by secretly marrying Natalia in the Orthodox Church in Vienna.

The Tsar also had four uncles. The Grand Duke Vladimir, according to one of the family, 'almost struck terror into Nicholas', and had the most confident opinions on everything from the ballet to politics; his son, the Grand Duke Cyril, committed the almost inexcusable error of marrying, without the Tsar's consent, Victoria Melita of Saxe-Coburg, who was not only his first cousin but had deserted and divorced the Tsarina's brother Alexander of Hesse. Another uncle was the incompetent and profligate Grand Duke Alexis who spent his last years amid the night clubs of Paris. The Grand Duke Sergius was perhaps the most difficult and overbearing of Nicholas's uncles, until he was removed by an assassin's bomb in 1905. The Tsar's youngest uncle, the Grand Duke Paul, affronted his nephew with yet another marriage to a divorcée, causing Nicholas to write despairingly to his mother, 'In the end, I fear, a whole colony of members of the Russian Imperial family will be established in Paris with their semi-legitimate and illegitimate wives. God alone knows what times we are living in when undisguised selfishness stifles all feelings of conscience, duty or even ordinary decency.'

The Tsar's numerous cousins were equally unmanageable. Perhaps excessive privilege and insufficient serious occupation were to blame. Certainly the Grand Duchess Olga was later to observe that for the Romanovs in general 'little mattered except the unending gratification of personal desire and ambition'. But Nicholas himself was in many ways an inadequate head of the family, avoiding frank confrontations and meting out fitful punishments apparently inspired by the Tsarina's notorious puritanism.

Family squabbles were soon dwarfed by the outbreak of the First World War. Russia went to war with Austria and Germany to protect the threatened Serbs and because mobilization against the former risked national security on the common frontier with Germany. The declaration of war was attended by a remarkable upsurge in the popularity of the monarchy: in St Petersburg (hastily renamed Petrograd, which sounded truly Russian and not German) and Moscow, tens of thousands gathered to salute the royal family and sing 'God Save the Tsar'. With the exception of the Bolsheviks, whose leaders were later arrested, the democratic and socialist parties in the Duma threw their weight behind the war effort, hoping for constitutional reforms later.

The Imperial family also rallied to the country's cause. Although the Tsar wanted to assume command at the front, the Grand Duke Nicholas Nicholaevich, his able and popular cousin, was made Commander-in-Chief. The Romanov womenfolk, like their British and German equivalents, visited wounded soldiers and even, on occasion, dressed wounds and assisted at operations.

Within a year of the outbreak of war the Russian forces had suffered nearly 3,000,000 casualties; though there had been early successes against the Austrians, the crushing German victories of Tannenberg and the Masurian Lakes had opened the way for humiliating Russian withdrawals in Poland and Lithuania. On 5 September 1915 the Tsar astounded world opinion by superseding the Grand Duke Nicholas as Russian Commander-in-Chief; in fact the Tsar interfered little in military decisions, and his main function was to show himself and, on occasion, the Tsarevich to officers and men at the front. Nicholas simultaneously made Alexandra his co-ruler, thus advancing the political influence of the durable Rasputin.

In December 1916, amid military confusion, political intrigue, strikes and food shortages, the Tsarina wrote forcefully to the Tsar:

85 *The Tsarina, Alexandra. She was only twenty-two, and Nicholas twenty-six, when he became Tsar, on his father's early death in 1894. 'What a terrible load of responsibility has been laid upon the poor children!' wrote Queen Victoria.*

86 *Tsar Nicholas II in naval uniform.*

87 *The waiting crowds outside the Ouspensky cathedral, in Moscow, where Nicholas and Alexandra were crowned with great pomp in May 1896.*

Draw the reins in tightly, which you let loose . . . Russia loves to feel the whip . . . Be the Emperor, be Peter the Great, Ivan the Terrible, the Emperor Paul – crush them all under you. Now don't you laugh, naughty one . . . I kiss you, caress you, long for you, can't sleep without you, bless you.

Nicholas replied meekly in English (the language they most often used together), 'Tender thanks for the severe written scolding. . . . Your poor little weak-willed hubby.'

In December 1916 Rasputin was murdered by a group of plotters including Prince Felix Yusupov, the Tsar's nephew-in-law, and the Grand Duke Dmitri Pavlovich, first cousin of Nicholas. Rasputin was lured to Yusupov's palace; there he consumed quantities of potassium cyanide contained in almond cakes and wine. As these lethal doses had no apparent effect upon the holy man Yusupov and a fellow-conspirator fired a large number of bullets into him and battered him with a heavy weapon; he was then dumped, still alive, into a canal where he eventually drowned. Rasputin's removal did not galvanize the Russian administration; Nicholas and Alexandra were not ousted.

In March 1917 the Tsar's authority crumbled around him as a war-weary nation demanded sweeping changes in the character of the government. As the military got out of hand and the Duma's clamour for a new constitution became irresistible, Nicholas decided, on 15 March, to abdicate in his own and in his son's name. Characteristically imperturbable amid these disasters, he provoked one of his staff officers to recall that 'he had abdicated from the throne of Russia as if he were handing over a squadron'.

The new Provisional Government was willing to allow Nicholas and his family to sail for England via Murmansk. The ex-Tsar's cousin George V offered asylum, but the Prime Minister Lloyd George was cool towards the idea. The Tsar's family were kept as prisoners at their favourite palace at Tsarskoe Selo, where their guards treated them with a mixture of deference and contempt. In July Kerensky became Prime Minister and decided to move the Imperial family. On 13 August they left on a long journey that was to take them to a small mansion at Tobolsk in Siberia. There Alexandra was consumed with bitterness for the nation's ingratitude towards her husband, while Nicholas seemed reasonably content with his depressed circumstances.

But in October 1917 came the Bolshevik Revolution, which overthrew Kerensky's regime to the accompaniment of the slogan 'Peace, land and bread'. The new government, dominated by Lenin and Trotsky, began to sue for peace. At Tobolsk the royal family were put on army rations early in 1918 and their allowance was cut, necessitating the dismissal of servants. To cap it all the ex-Tsarevich injured his groin and suffered an agonizing haemorrhage that crippled him for the remaining period of his life.

In April 1918 the family were taken to Ekaterinburg, some three hundred miles southeast of Tobolsk. Rumours of rescue plots multiplied, while members of the Ekaterinburg Soviet talked of killing the Imperial family which was an obvious rallying point for counter-revolutionary forces. At Ipatiev House, in Ekaterinburg, authority had passed to the commissar Alexander Avdeyev, who ordered his men to keep a close and sometimes crude watch on their captives. Some of the guards found Nicholas kindly, simple and talkative, while Alexandra was considered haughty and solemn.

In June Avdeyev was dismissed and the guards were changed. On 12 July 1918 the Imperial family were ordered into the half-basement by the new commissar Jacob Yurovsky, who subsequently appeared with several guards. He then read out a brief order of execution from the Ekaterinburg Soviet, and the ex-Tsar and his family were murdered with bullets and bayonets. Lenin's government denied its responsibility for the murders, but there was no doubt that the new regime had wanted the Imperial family out of the way.

Other Romanovs were hunted down in Russia, but approximately half of the family survived. The dowager Empress Marie eventually arrived in England to be welcomed by her sister Alexandra the Queen Mother; the Grand Duchess Xenia followed her. Others made their way to France, to Switzerland and to the United States. The Grand Duke Cyril proclaimed himself Tsar in France in 1924, and eventually identified his cause with that of Italian fascism. In 1938 a small stir was caused when Cyril's daughter Kira married Louis Ferdinand, son of the former Crown Prince of Germany – but neither Hohenzollerns nor Romanovs were to see their crowns restored.

One of the most interesting aspects of the fall of the Romanovs has been the claims of various pretenders to be members of the murdered family. The most persistent and remarkable is the claim of one Anna Anderson that she was the Tsar's youngest daughter Anastasia; some members of the Romanov family championed her cause, but it aroused much scepticism among others; certainly she was never allowed to lay hands on whatever Romanov funds existed in England and Germany. There have also been claimants posing as the Tsarevich Alexis, and even Nicholas II has been 'sighted' by some eccentrics.

Genuine Romanov survivors of the Revolution have played an active part in American and European high society; their exploits have kept the gossip columnists happy, and television, the cinema and other organs of the mass media have used Romanov memoirs and experiences profitably enough. But the Romanovs no longer aspire to rise again on the ruins of the Soviet state, and in 1961 their changed circumstances were neatly symbolized by the return to Russia, as a British tourist, of Prince Alexander, a great-nephew of Nicholas II, who went camera in hand to see the glories of the Winter Palace and the Kremlin.

88 (Above, opposite) Tsar Nicholas's children. Left to right: the Grand Duchesses Maria, Olga, Anastasia and Tatiana and the Tsarevich Alexis.

89 (Below, opposite) The haemophiliac Tsarevich with his Sicilian donkey cart, a present from the King of Italy. Alexis, though he looked and behaved like a normal boy, often had to spend weeks in bed in what was frequently appalling pain. The nature of his illness was kept secret.

90 Nicholas's mother, the elegant Dowager Tsarina Marie, with her sister, Queen Alexandra of England, standing on the steps of their Danish home, Villa Hvidore in Copenhagen.

91 Nicholas and the Tsarevich at the front during the 1914–18 war. At first the war brought a sharp increase of popularity for the Tsar.

92 (Below) The Tsar's four daughters, Olga, Maria, Tatiana and Anastasia. They would often write their letters jointly and sign them O.M.T.A.

93 (Overleaf) The Tsar, the Tsarevich and the four Grand Duchesses, photographed with a group of Cossack officers just before the Revolution of 1917.

94 (Left) The Tsar in Berlin in 1913 with his cousin, George V of England (right). The two men were very much alike and were often mistaken for one another.

95 (Right) The constitutional reforms of 1905 brought Nicholas little credit; his position was threatened by the disastrous failures of the Russo-Japanese war, and the unpopularity of 'the German woman' Alexandra, and her confidant the sinister Rasputin. This clay caricature of Nicholas was one of many which were being sold all over Paris in 1910.

96 *(Left) The Tsar and the Kaiser together in 1914.*

97 *(Above) The Tsar would not hear a word against
Alexandra or Rasputin. In spring 1917 he went back to the*
*front, leaving the Tsarina in complete control of government.
The photograph shows Nicholas arriving at the Russian
General Headquarters.*

98 Nicholas inspecting the Tscherkasky Regiment. His chief role in military matters was to put in appearances; he interfered little with military decisions.

99 (Below) Another of Nicholas's appearances, which were supposed to keep up the morale of the troops. Here he gives the troops his blessing, with a holy icon in his hand.

100 *Nicholas revelled in the grand ceremonial parades, knowing that his power was based on the army. Here army officers cheer the Tsar after a review on the great military plain near Moscow.*

101 (Left) Rasputin, the disreputable monk. He controlled the Imperial family through his apparent ability to relieve the sufferings of the Tsarevich.

102 A haunting picture of Alexandra with the Tsarevich. 'Think of the torture of that mother, an impotent witness of her son's martyrdom,' wrote Pierre Gilliar, the boy's tutor.

103 (Below) Rasputin's hypnotic eyes and peasant earthiness brought him remarkable success with the ladies. This photograph shows him with a group of admirers.

104 *Rasputin holding court. He did not trouble to conceal his debauchery; many, who did not know the secret of the Tsarevich's illness and thus could not account for Rasputin's hold over Alexandra, believed that he was the Tsarina's lover.*

105 *(Below left) Prince Felix Yusupov, married to the Tsar's niece. With his cousin Dmitri Pavlovich and other plotters he murdered Rasputin in an attempt to save the Romanov dynasty from destruction.*

106 *(Below right) Prince Felix Yusupov in 1966, at the age of 79. He has written vivid accounts of Rasputin's murder.*

107 The Bolsheviks overthrew the Provisional Government under Kerensky in October 1917. This photograph shows the Bolsheviks marching through St Petersburg; their slogan was 'peace, land and bread'.

108 (Below) Looting and destruction in 1917, with the army joining the mob.

109 (Right) The Tsar under arrest at his palace of Tsarskoe Selo, after his abdication on 15 March 1917. The abdication took place in the drawing-room car of the Imperial train, drawn up at Pskov.

110 *A somewhat forbidding Alexandra, imprisoned at Tsarskoe Selo, continues to do her needlework sitting in her wheel chair.*

111 *(Right) Kerensky and the Provisional Government moved the Imperial family from Tsarskoe Selo to Tobolsk, in Siberia, on 14 April 1917, in order to protect them from the hotheads among the Soviet, an assembly of workers' and soldiers' deputies which was sharing power with the Duma. At Tobolsk the family still lived in reasonable comfort. This photograph shows them modestly dressed and sitting on the roof of the house that was their prison.*

112 Grand Duchess Xenia of Russia, Nicholas's sister, who escaped to England in 1919 with her children. She came to live at Hampton Court, where this photograph was taken.

113 (Above right, opposite) Prince Alexander Romanov at a charity stall in London. He is a great-nephew of Nicholas, but in 1961 was able to visit Moscow as a British tourist.

114 (Below right, opposite) This cable, sent to Princess Victoria by Grand Duchess Xenia on her arrival in Malta following her escape from Russia, shows (despite the seven bedrooms) how far the Romanovs had fallen from their imperial splendour.

Princess Victoria
Marlborough House
London

Leaving tomorrow. Please take
seven bedrooms two servants
rooms one sitting & dining rooms
cheapest possible hôtel.
Divine here. Written.

Xenia

Chapter Four

The Latin Monarchies

Portugal

The Portuguese monarchy survived exactly one decade of the twentieth century. To some foreign observers it seemed strange that a monarchy that could trace its roots back to the Middle Ages, that had enjoyed a tradition of alliance with the crown of England since 1386 and the days of John of Gaunt, and could boast such illustrious rulers as Prince Henry the Navigator and John II, should fall so easily.

In fact, the financial extravagance and generally uninspiring deportment of the House of Bragança during the second half of the nineteenth century had caused widespread resentment. In 1890, furthermore, the British government, backing up Cecil Rhodes's private expansion into Central Africa, had brusquely demanded that Portugal withdraw from Nyasaland and Mashonaland. Portugal's humiliation was blamed upon the monarchy by republican elements. Moreover, in 1889 the Brazilian branch of the Braganças had been overthrown; the fall of the Emperor of Brazil also shook the Portuguese throne. In January 1891 a small body of mutinous troops actually seized the city hall at Oporto, though the uprising was quickly suppressed. The Portuguese government also had to wrestle with a series of financial crises during which it seemed likely that Portugal's two most desirable African colonies (Angola and Mozambique) might have to be pawned to foreign creditor nations – notably Britain; in 1898, in fact, Britain and Germany came to an agreement to share any future provision of financial aid to Portugal, with Mozambique allotted as security for Britain and Angola for Germany.

Somehow the Portuguese government survived its embarrassing indebtedness, though by 1900 it owed some £177,000,000 (or £35 per head of population, the heaviest debt per head anywhere outside of Australasia). The inevitable prominence in Portuguese affairs of foreign bankers and financiers enabled the republicans to accuse the royal family of being a foreign dynasty or, at the very least, too closely linked with external creditors. The House of Bragança robustly denied these aspersions, and King Carlos I, who reigned until 1908, did his best to counteract his stout Germanic appearance (possibly acquired from his grandfather, Ferdinand of Saxe-Coburg-Gotha) by playing the role of an Alentejo landowner and wearing provincial costume. The republicans also accused the court of personal extravagance and therefore of contributing to the country's financial plight; these charges were, on the whole, unfounded, since the royal family lived fairly modestly and without financial excess.

By 1906, however, the anti-monarchist movement was growing rapidly in strength. There were mass meetings and defections of leading monarchists, and in the 1906 elections the republicans polled over half the votes in Lisbon. In April of that year there were mutinies on the warships *Don Carlos* and *Vasco da Gama*. As monarchist politicians struggled to hold on to power by the questionable expedients of muzzling the republican press and modifying

115 Queen Marie Pia of Portugal, mother of King Carlos.
The Portuguese royal family at this time had a reputation for
financial extravagance and uninspiring deportment.

the electoral laws, attacks on the crown multiplied. In November 1906 it was revealed that illegal financial advances had been made to the King from the Treasury without the consent of the Cortes (the Portuguese parliament).

In May 1907 the monarchist Prime Minister João Franco dissolved the Cortes and announced that he would govern by decree. King Carlos backed up this open dictatorship, thus losing the support of those monarchists who deplored despotic rule. On 6 January 1908 the royal family left Lisbon for their palace at Vila Viçosa. Meanwhile João Franco uncovered a republican plan for an uprising; he arrested republican leaders and drew up a decree applying the penalty of transportation for life for crimes against the security of the state. King Carlos signed the decree and decided to return to Lisbon; on 1 February en route for Lisbon the King and his heir Prince Luis Filipe were assassinated by republicans.

Carlos was succeeded by his inexperienced and shaken younger son, who became King Manuel II at the age of eighteen. He was shored up by his determined mother, Queen Amelia, daughter of the French pretender the Count of Paris. The Council of State met at the palace in Lisbon, and Manuel carried out its recommendation to dismiss Franco. But both within the Cortes, which was reopened in March 1909, and in the cities and towns anti-monarchical feeling grew. Sedition flourished in the navy and in the Lisbon garrison.

In October 1910 a somewhat inefficiently organized revolution broke out; two rebellious warships bombarded the royal palace at Lisbon on 4 October; the royalist element in the armed forces failed to rally to the monarchy. Eventually Manuel II and his family fled to the fishing village of Ericeira where they boarded the royal yacht. After toying with the idea of making for Oporto the King decided to sail for Gibraltar. Within a year Portugal was officially a republic, and like so many other exiles Manuel settled in Britain. He and his family went to live at Fulwell Park in Twickenham, where the ex-King devoted much of his time to building a magnificent collection of Portuguese books. The last King of Portugal died in exile in 1932.

116 King Luis, Carlos's father.

117 (Right) Luis Filipe, Carlos's eldest son, who was assassinated with his father by republicans in February 1908.

118 Carlos I. Stout and Germanic in appearance, he tried to identify himself with the Portuguese landowners, frequently dressing in provincial costume.

119 (Below left) The Infanta Maria das Neves of Portugal. Infanta Maria was decorated by the Austrian government for her bravery under fire after two years' Red Cross nursing with the Austrian army during the First World War.

120 (Above right) Queen Amelia, Carlos's wife and the daughter of the French pretender, the Count of Paris. After the assassination of her husband and eldest son, Amelia made a determined attempt to bolster up her second son, Manuel II, when he came to the throne at the age of eighteen, but the Bragança dynasty failed to survive and Manuel fled the country after only two years as king.

121 (Below right) Manuel II's wife, the former Princess Augustine Victoria of Hohenzollern, whom he married after leaving Portugal. She and Manuel lived for many years at Fulwell Park in Twickenham with their family.

122 (Opposite) An official portrait of Manuel II, Portugal's last king. He died in 1932.

123 *One of the last photographs taken of King Manuel before his exile.*

124 *(Below) King Manuel making his first public appearance as King.*

125 *(Right) Looking relaxed in exile, Manuel and his future bride, Princess Augustine Victoria of Hohenzollern, are chaperoned by her father, Prince Wilhelm of Hohenzollern.*

Spain

In a sense, Alfonso XIII became King of Spain in his mother's womb. When his father Alfonso XII died in 1885 he left behind his widowed Queen, Maria Cristina of Austria, and two young daughters. But Maria Cristina was pregnant, and six months after her husband's death she gave birth to a son, the future Alfonso XIII. As the cannon triumphantly crashed out a twenty-one-gun salute, the Prime Minister Sagasta appeared before the assembled court carrying a silver tray on which lay naked the new King of Spain. Five days later the baby was carried in solemn procession, with the golden fleece around his neck, to be baptised in the Royal Chapel with water brought specially from the River Jordan.

The regency of Alfonso XIII survived threats from the republicans and from other branches of the Spanish Bourbon family – particularly from the Carlists, the descendants of Don Carlos (1788–1855) who had challenged his niece Isabella's right to ascend the throne in 1833. Until he was seven the infant King's life was divided between the royal palaces in Madrid and the seaside resort of San Sebastian where his mother had a holiday residence called Miramar. Fearing that Alfonso had inherited his father's tubercular condition, Maria Cristina ensured that he spent most of his time at Miramar out of doors; his health proved excellent in this open-air regime. While staying at Miramar the royal family was once visited by Queen Victoria, who drove over from nearby Biarritz and found the tea that she was offered by Maria Cristina almost undrinkable.

The young King's education began seriously when he reached the age of seven. He was taught French, English, German, Italian, physics, chemistry, military and general history, geography and literature. He showed considerable aptitude for these lessons, particularly for history and literature, though he also became an excellent linguist. He loved physical exercise, riding, sailing, swimming and military drill. Apparently he inherited his father's caustic sense of humour, for once when he had been locked in his room for some misdemeanour he flung open the shutters of his window and called out angrily to those in the courtyard below, '*Viva la república! Viva la república!*'

The dynasty survived the shock of the humiliating loss of Cuba and the Philippines as a result of the brief war with the United States in 1898, and in 1902 Alfonso attained the age of sixteen and was formally proclaimed King. He straightway drove to the Cortes where the whole assembly burst into applause as he entered in the full-dress uniform of a captain-general. Once enthroned he took his oath on the Bible: 'I swear by God, on the Holy Gospels, to keep the Constitution and the Laws. If I do so God reward me for it, and if not, may He ask me to give account.' On returning to the palace Alfonso received his ministers' formal offers of resignation and confirmed them in their posts. This was expected; what was not expected was his immediate demand to hold a council there and then. Alfonso's first council was a stormy affair: he berated the Minister of War for closing the military academies and read out a clause of the Constitution to back up his arguments. His troubled ministers realized that here was an awkward new force at the centre of power, but they contented themselves with reminding their sovereign that all his commands had to be countersigned by a minister.

In 1906 Alfonso married Princess Ena of Battenberg, a grand-daughter of Queen Victoria. Having unobtrusively accepted the Catholic faith, Ena was married to the King in the Church of San Jeronimo in Madrid. As the royal couple were returning to the Palacio Real an anarchist called Mateo Morral threw a bomb at their coach; the explosion killed twelve onlookers and wounded a hundred more, as well as maiming some horses. As Alfonso led his shaken bride out of their carriage, her shoes and the train of her dress were stained with blood. The ceremonials, however, continued and the Prince of Wales (the future George V) proposed their health at the state luncheon, later confessing that it was 'not easy after the emotions caused by this terrible affair'.

The ominous portents of Alfonso and Ena's wedding-day were amply confirmed by subsequent events. The new Queen transmitted haemophilia to the first and the fourth of the four sons she bore Alfonso; only the third son, Don Juan, was bodily sound, for the second son was born a deaf-mute; two healthy daughters were born, however, since haemophilia only manifests itself in male progeny. Even these misfortunes do not seem to have blunted Alfonso's zest, impulsiveness, quickness of mind, or his taste for imperious commands. His pastimes were essentially those of a man of action, particularly his chosen sports of fast motoring, shooting, yachting and horse racing. His cultural interests were decidedly pedestrian.

Spain remained neutral during the First World War, though Alfonso and Ena personally supported the Allies, as did the Carlist pretender to the throne, Don Jaime. When the war ended Alfonso made an imprudent bid to bolster Spain's military reputation by crushing the Moors in the protectorate of Morocco. The King had always cherished his army and delighted in treating them to impassioned speeches recalling past Spanish glories. Doubtless he also hoped that a spectacular success in Morocco would strengthen his hand against the politicians, and in May 1921 he made a speech at Cordoba denouncing the Spanish parliamentary system. But Alfonso's army in Morocco blundered to a terrible defeat a few months later; 10,000 troops were slaughtered, and republicans were quick to blame the King for promoting this calamity.

Against a background of republican agitation, civil disturbance, strikes, bombings and general discontent, General Primo de Rivera planned a militarist coup d'état in 1923. After all, Mussolini had recently overthrown parliamentary government in Italy, and Spain would no doubt benefit from a similar upheaval. In September 1923 de Rivera acted; martial law was declared, and the King was called upon to dismiss his government and rule with the help of the army. The coup was welcome news to Alfonso, and he hastened to confirm General de Rivera in power. Despite protests, the Cortes was not recalled and when, two months after setting up the military dictatorship, Alfonso and Ena paid a state visit to Italy, the King proudly introduced de Rivera as 'my Mussolini'.

So Alfonso had now stolen the clothes of the Carlists, not that the Carlist claimant Don Jaime seems to have cared much for his cause. The King also drew further away from his wife, and soon Madrid was full of rumours of his infidelities. Queen Ena's life was a compound of the most stultified ceremonial, such as the symbolic washing of the feet of twelve old, poor women at Easter time, and routine good works – like working for the Red Cross Hospital in Madrid. Even her private pastimes were not wholly her own: she scandalized conservative Spanish opinion by wearing a tight-fitting bathing costume at San Sebastian, and when she swam two fully-armed and uniformed soldiers waded in beside her.

Bodyguards were an essential part of the royal family's life, and few months passed without assassination plots against the King being discovered. In 1930 he rid himself of his weary dictator de Rivera and disassociated himself from his work. Alfonso still lived the dashing, sporty life of a playboy, even in his mid-forties, thus prompting a critic to remark,

▶111

27 Alfonso XIII of Spain, sporting an exotic species of
plus-fours, was photographed in the Highlands of Scotland
while staying with the Duke of Sutherland.

128 Isabella II, Queen of Spain 1830–1904.

129 *A cadaverous Alfonso at Osborne with his wife, Princess Victoria Eugenie of Battenberg, always known as Princess Ena. Her fair hair, blue eyes and rosy cheeks* appealed to the Spanish, who called her 'la Reina hermosa' – the beautiful Queen.

130 (Left) Ena as Queen of Spain with her daughters, Princess Beatrice (right) and Princess Maria Cristina. Ena was a carrier of haemophilia and only one of her four sons was healthy; two were haemophiliacs and one was a deaf-mute.

131 Queen Ena in the last year of Alfonso's reign, at an anti-tubercular dispensary in Madrid. She was expected to take part in good works, but her presence seems to have intimidated these infants.

132 (Below) Queen Ena in her riding habit, shaking hands with the Infanta Louisa. Ena was happiest out of doors; she loved swimming, riding and playing golf, though protocol sometimes intervened – when she swam she was accompanied by armed guards!

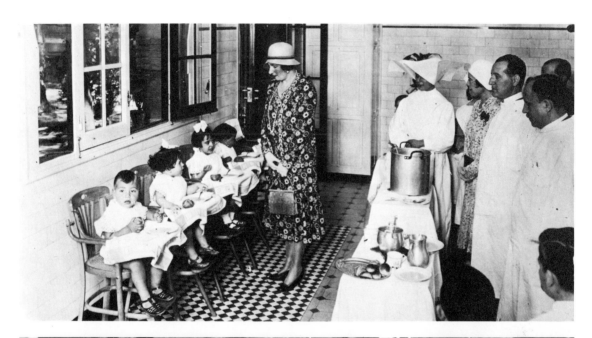

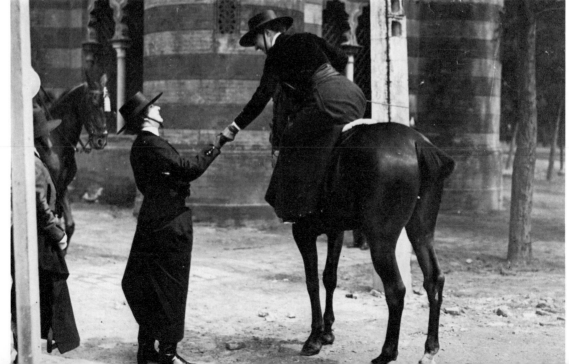

133 The Prince of the Asturias, the haemophiliac heir to the Spanish throne. The photograph shows him flanked by his six tutors and his spiritual adviser. In fact the Prince survived for some time; he was twice married and twice divorced and eventually died following a car crash in Miami.

134 Don Juan of Spain (third son of Alfonso) and his wife.
Don Juan was charming, popular and above all healthy.
He married Princess Maria-Mercedes of Bourbon-Sicily in
1935, and their son, Don Juan Carlos, succeeded to the
Spanish throne in November 1975 following Franco's death.

135 (Far left) Queen Ena. Her looks and elegance were much admired. 'She embodies the ideal of beautiful English womanhood,' wrote Alfonso's aunt, the Infanta Eulalia; Lady Duff Gordon said that had Queen Ena been born into another walk of life she could have made her fortune as a couturière.

136 Alfonso and his heir, the Prince of the Asturias, sharing family fun.

137 (Above left) In exile Alfonso did not lose his zest for living. He settled in France, near Fontainebleau, where he organized numerous activities such as this tennis match.

138 Alfonso's aged aunt, the Infanta Isabel, who died in Paris, three days after going into exile.

139 (Below) Maria-Mercedes, the wife of Don Juan, having her portrait painted by a shifty-looking del Camino. When this photograph was published it caused a scandal, for in the unfinished portrait the Princess appears to be semi-naked.

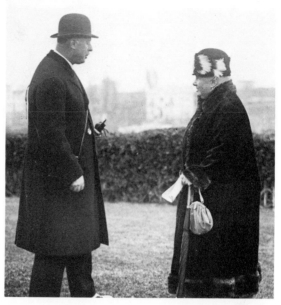

140 (Above left) On 23 July 1966 Don Juan Carlos took his oath in the Cortes at Madrid as the successor to the head of state. On the right is General Franco.

141 (Below left) In August 1959 Don Juan (left) and his son Don Juan Carlos dined at a Red Cross Gala in Monaco with Princess Grace.

142 Don Juan Carlos with his wife, Princess Sophia of Greece, and their children, Felipe, Elena and Cristina, at their home, the Zarzuela Palace in Madrid.

143 Victor Emmanuel II of Savoy, the first King of modern Italy, who instituted a constitutional monarchy inherited from Piedmont.

144 The aggressively moustachioed King Humbert I of Italy, whose reactionary attitudes did much to undermine the prestige of the House of Savoy. He was assassinated in 1900 by Gaetano Bresci.

145 Queen Margherita, beautiful wife and cousin of Humbert I.

146 The Duchess of Aosta, arrogant and affected, was said to behave as though she were the real sovereign of Italy.

'Chronic adolescence may be permissible in certain walks of life, but in the ruler it is distinctly out of place.' Doubtless this frenetic activity was in part a compensation for the disappointments of family life; despairing of his two haemophiliac sons, the Prince of the Asturias and Don Gonzalo, and of the deaf-mute Don Jaime, the King's hopes were centred on the charming and intelligent Don Juan; the two healthy Infantas were no substitute for a pack of strong sons.

Civil discontent in Spain burgeoned during 1930, and on all sides men called for a republic and a return to democracy. In 1931 Alfonso was forced to agree to municipal elections and elections to the Cortes. The municipal election results showed staggering early successes for the republicans; soon republican crowds were in the streets demanding Alfonso's abdication. The King had no choice now but to leave Spain, but he refused to abdicate or renounce his rights – which he described as 'a deposit accumulated by history'.

The Spanish royal family scattered to different parts of Europe, and Alfonso and Ena agreed to separate. The ex-King spent a good deal of his time in travel and frivolous activity. In 1934 his son Don Jaime married, and his youngest son, the haemophiliac Don Gonzalo, died in Austria from a haemorrhage following a car crash. In 1935 Don Juan married Maria-Mercedes of Bourbon-Sicily, having completed his training in the British Royal Navy. The two Infantas, Beatrice and Maria Cristina, married Italian aristocrats. The Prince of the Asturias married twice and got divorced twice (in Cuba); he eventually bled to death after crashing his car into a tree in Miami; a cigarette girl called 'Merry Mildred' Gaydon was at his side but lived to attend his funeral in Florida.

The Spanish Civil War of 1936–9 destroyed the republic, but Generalissimo Franco chose not to restore the monarchy – either Carlist or Bourbon. Alfonso died in Rome in 1941, having renounced his rights in favour of his son Don Juan. The ensuing years brought some comfort to Spanish monarchists, since Don Juan Carlos, son of the allegedly liberal Don Juan, was eventually named as heir to the vacant golden throne of Spain. In 1974, during Franco's severe illness, Don Juan Carlos assumed the Caudillo's powers, only to lose them when the latter staged a miraculous recovery. In November 1975, however, death finally claimed Franco, and on 22 November Juan Carlos I was sworn in as king in a fifty-minute ceremony in Madrid. He and his Queen, Sophia of Greece, face an uncertain future.

Italy

King Victor Emmanuel III ascended the throne of Italy in 1900 after the assassination of his father King Humbert I by Gaetano Bresci, a revolutionary and an anarchist. The dead King had contributed a great deal to the decline in the prestige of the House of Savoy by his reactionary attitudes and his insistence on moving within a narrow court circle. The new King, who was destined to reign until the traumatic year of 1946, was reckoned to be a supporter of liberal measures, and a hard and conscientious worker with a high ideal of his royal office.

In his first public speech after his accession Victor Emmanuel III told the senate in Rome that he 'would never be lacking in the serenest faith in the liberal order', thus clearly dedicating himself to the restoration of the constitutional monarchy inherited from Piedmont and supported by his grandfather, Victor Emmanuel II (1820–78). It was ironic that the new King, having been hailed as the white hope of liberals and socialists, should have confirmed

Mussolini in office in 1922 as the head of a fascist and extreme nationalist coalition government, and thus opened the way to more than twenty years of extreme right-wing rule.

Victor Emmanuel III was extraordinarily short of stature, whereas by contrast his cousin Emmanuel Philibert, Duke of Aosta, was imposing and regal. One of the King's later Prime Ministers, Francesco Nitti, recalled the comparison between the two leading males of the House of Savoy, and their wives:

The little King was unaffected, taciturn, dedicated to scholarly pursuits, modest and without any pretensions, yet intelligent and very erudite. But the Duke of Aosta appeared much more imposing and majestic, although he never found a way to demonstrate his own intellectual accomplishments, which in fact were strictly non-existent. The Queen [Elena of Montenegro], although born in a small Balkan village, the daughter of a very minor, luckless prince, was beautiful, regal, and modest, while the Duchess of Aosta, who believed herself to be heiress to the grandeur of the Bourbons of France and proudly signed her name Hélène de France . . . was affected and loved to behave as if she were the real sovereign.

From 1896 to 1901 Victor Emmanuel and his wife remained childless, and the Queen Mother Margherita was convinced that, though they were obviously devoted to each other, perhaps 'too much thinking about it . . . is harmful to the realization of the desire!' In June 1901, however, a daughter was born and christened Yolanda Margherita; the following year a second daughter, Mafalda, was born. Then in 1904, at a tenth-century castle in Piedmont, the Queen was delivered of a son who weighed ten pounds and resembled his dark-haired mother; batteries of guns blazed away to announce the birth of a direct heir to the throne. Humbert was destined to grow into a tall, handsome and elegant man, and to become the last King of Italy for thirty-four days in 1946; his character was not untarnished, however, and there were insistent rumours of his skirt-chasing profligate ways and his alleged homosexuality. Despite these aspersions, Humbert married Maria José, daughter of the King of the Belgians, in 1930 and fathered four children (one boy and three girls), though the first two children were conceived after artificial insemination. Two more daughters were born to Victor Emmanuel and Elena: Giovanna, in 1907 (who was later to marry the Tsar of Bulgaria) and Maria, in 1914.

The royal children were brought up in an extremely unpretentious domestic environment. They lived mostly in the modest Villa Ada, surrounded by ten acres of forest and meadowland, near Rome. They had few servants; Elena enjoyed cooking and even cleaning; Victor Emmanuel hunted, tended his flowers, and toyed with his coin collection. Each morning the King was driven to 'his office', the Quirinal Palace. The court at the Quirinal was somewhat bourgeois, restrained and austere, and the King gained some pleasure from slighting members of the ancient aristocracy. Victor Emmanuel had no desire to be closely associated with Italian high society, which he considered to be obsessed with horse-racing and cluttered with divorcees.

Having seen his country win substantial territorial concessions from Austria during the First World War, Victor Emmanuel accepted Mussolini's rise to power as, at the worst, a protection against Bolshevik revolution. Revelling in the law and order and the national efficiency imposed by *Il Duce*, the King was prepared to see his constitutional position by-passed and eroded. His elevation to Imperial status by the brutal conquest of Abyssinia in

1936 overjoyed him, and Queen Elena gave her gold wedding-ring to be melted down in support of the campaign.

Despite some misgivings over the Rome–Berlin Axis, Victor Emmanuel briskly supported his country's entry into the Second World War, donning military uniform in the well-established Savoyard tradition. But the war did not bring military glory to the country; Italian troops were humiliatingly ejected from Greece, and suffered disastrous defeats in East and North Africa. In 1943 the King and Marshal Badoglio engineered a coup that forced Mussolini's resignation; the fallen *Duce* was imprisoned but was dramatically rescued by German parachutists two months later. Mussolini then set up a republican fascist government administering German-occupied northern Italy. Finally, as the Allies advanced from the south and anti-fascist forces reconquered the north, Mussolini was captured by partisans and shot on the shores of Lake Como.

Under Anglo-American pressure the King decided in 1944 to retire from public affairs; he did not abdicate, however, though Crown Prince Humbert exercised all the functions of the Crown. In May 1946 Victor Emmanuel abdicated in favour of his son. King Humbert's reign was soon ended when a referendum resulted in twelve million votes for a republic against ten million votes for the monarchy. After a thousand years the House of Savoy no longer had subjects to rule.

Victor Emmanuel died in Alexandria in 1947, having devoted his last months to stamp-collecting, fishing, and strolling in the garden of his villa; he was buried in a Catholic church in Alexandria. Ex-Queen Elena went to Montpellier, where she died of cancer in 1952. Humbert retired to Portugal, as did his sister Giovanna, former Tsarina of Bulgaria; his wife, Maria José, left him in 1946 and went to live in Switzerland where she wrote a book about the first Duke of Savoy.

There seems little likelihood that Humbert's son Victor Emmanuel, pretender to the crown of Italy, will be restored; indeed he has exhibited little desire for such a restoration. Amid the rise and fall of Italian governments, the House of Savoy can claim little contemporary relevance. The throne upon which its kings once sat is now in a museum in Turin; it seems destined to remain there.

147 Queen Elena, the wife of Victor Emmanuel III. She enjoyed being a housewife at the royal home, the Villa Ada near Rome.

148 (Right) Victor Emmanuel III, two years after he became King. He was the white hope of the liberals on his accession, but in 1922 confirmed Mussolini in office at the head of a fascist government.

149 (Above right, opposite) Meeting of tiny men. Victor Emmanuel at an exhibition of Japanese art in Rome was saluted by the Japanese who accompanied the exhibits.

150 (Below right, opposite) The diminutive King on a visit to Montenegro (his wife's birthplace) early in his reign. An enthusiastic photographer, he nearly always took his camera on his travels.

151 *Victor Emmanuel at a review. He supported Italy's entry into the Second World War, donning military uniform in the well-established Savoyard tradition.*

152 *(Below) In uniform again, Victor Emmanuel shakes hands with military attachés from Nazi Germany.*

153 *(Above right) In 1936 the King made part of a bored audience for the presentation of the Mussolini Prizes at the Italian Academy. This was the year of the Abyssinian campaign.*

154 *(Below right) Italy enters the war. The King with Mussolini in June 1940, with a group of officers.*

155 (Far left) The King's only son, Humbert, married Maria José, the Belgian King's daughter, in Turin on 8 January 1930. In spite of rumours that Humbert was homosexual, they had four children. Humbert became Italy's last King, reigning for thirty-four days.

156 (Left) Ex-King Humbert with Maria José in 1959, at their home in Merlinge.

157 (Above left) Maria José at her home with her daughter, Maria Pia, and her son-in-law, Prince Alexander of Yugoslavia, in 1959.

158 (Below left) Ex-King Humbert's son, Prince Victor Emmanuel, at home with his books in Merlinge.

159–60 Humbert's rebellious youngest daughter, Princess Maria Beatrice (left, scowling). Her father disapproved of her being photographed in her bikini; in 1967 she eloped to England with an actor, who was unable to stay long enough for them to be married.

Chapter Five

The Balkan Monarchies

Albania

The Albanian state was created out of the Turkish possessions in Europe during the Balkan Wars of 1912–13. Though the population was seventy per cent Moslem after being under Turkish rule from the late fifteenth century, it acquired a German ruler, Prince Wilhelm of Wied, after it was made an independent principality. Wilhelm's translation to a distant and brand-new throne was in keeping with the nineteenth-century practice of finding German princelings, who were acceptable to the great European powers, to establish new dynasties. But within six months of accepting the crown, Wilhelm left, baffled and defeated by his principality's internal chaos. The dissent between monarchists and parliamentarians, big landowners and peasants, Moslems and Orthodox Christians, meant that by December 1914 there were six regimes each claiming to be the legitimate government.

During the First World War Albania saw valuable frontier regions snatched by Greece, Montenegro and Serbia. Italian troops landed near Valona in October 1914 to protect their national interests; French forces had also been sent to the country by the end of the war. President Wilson of the United States, with his resolute advocacy of national self-determination, would not, however, accept the demand for the partition of Albania between Italy, Greece and Yugoslavia which arose in the immediate post-war period. The Albanians finally rid themselves of direct foreign intervention by expelling Italian forces in 1920.

A period of internal conflict between reformers and conservatives and between Moslems and Orthodox Christians led to the emergence of Ahmed Bey Zogu, one of Albania's largest landowners, as the country's master during 1925. He was elected President of the Republic in January 1925, thus superseding the Council of Regency that had been established in 1921. In March of the same year he adapted the constitution to give him increased personal power, and on 1 December 1928 he felt able to assume the title of King Zog.

King Zog's rise to power, however, was overshadowed by growing Italian influence. Italian financiers had established the National Bank of Albania, and soon the economic direction of the country was in Italian hands. Ideally King Zog would have liked to have steered an independent course between Italy and Yugoslavia, but this proved impossible. Italian domination eventually led to Mussolini's invasion of Albania in April 1939; Zog fled to neighbouring Greece and passed into exile, while his country was incorporated into the Italian kingdom.

When the Axis powers were finally ejected from Albania, the monarchy was not restored. The Communists, led by Enver Hoxha, came to power during the last year of the Second World War, and there was no likelihood of a restoration of the monarchy; a republic was proclaimed in January 1946. King Zog and his Queen were thus confirmed in the status of exiles. The fallen King must have gained some small satisfaction, however, from attending ex-King Victor Emmanuel's funeral in Alexandria in 1947, for, though vanquished in war, Zog had outlived his former adversary at the last.

161 Prince Wilhelm of Wied, the insignificant prince who was thought suitable by the European powers to become King of the newly created state of Albania in 1913. He left after six months, baffled by Albanian politics.

162 (Left) A dapper King Zog, formerly Ahmed Bey Zogu. Zog was an important Albanian landowner who came to power in 1925 and assumed the title of King Zog in 1928.

163 King Zog with his wife, Queen Geraldine, at their wedding in 1938. Next year Mussolini invaded Albania and the King and Queen fled into exile.

164 (Below) Geraldine in exile.

165 (Left) Shades of interwar Hollywood! King Zog's sister Princess Sania married a diplomat and lived in Paris.

166 Zog, magnificent in a white uniform, with four members of his staff.

167 (Below) In 1949 King Zog (bearing a superficial resemblance to Salvador Dali) and Queen Geraldine (second from left) attended a banquet held in Cairo to celebrate the 37th anniversary of Albania's independence. The ladies are Zog's sisters, Princess Sania, Majida and Muzayaj.

168 In 1929, a year after becoming King, Zog reviewed a company of irregulars at Tirana.

169 (Below) King Zog's palace at Tirana in 1931.

170 (Right) In 1961 some exiled Albanians in Paris actually proclaimed Zog's heir King Leka I of Albania. The photograph shows 22-year-old Leka taking the oath on the red flag with the black eagle.

Bulgaria

In 1887, following the unification of the provinces of Bulgaria and Eastern Roumelia, the Bulgarian Sobranjie (parliament) offered the newly united nation's shaky throne to Prince Ferdinand of Saxe-Coburg, an officer in the Imperial Austrian army. Few expected Prince Ferdinand's reign to last for long, despite his family connections with Queen Victoria's dead, lamented Albert; Russia disliked the way in which Bulgaria had recently been united; Ferdinand was a German Catholic amid a sea of Orthodox Slavs; the newly created state had little institutional permanence. Despite these apparently crippling handicaps, Ferdinand remained on the throne until 1918, when he handed over to his son Boris. Ferdinand in fact lived to attain the age of ninety-one, and when he died in 1950 the Communists had been in power for four years.

Ferdinand's considerable dynastic success was due in great measure to his capacity to trim his policies; under him the Bulgarian ship of state became a light, manoeuvrable, adaptable vessel, able to show a clean pair of heels to any adversaries. Thus Bulgaria tried to avoid too close a contact with any of the great power blocs of Eastern Europe. Ferdinand maintained his contacts with the Austrian court and the Hungarian aristocracy after he moved to Sofia. He seemed at first determined to maintain his western contacts, chiefly to counteract the looming presence of Mother Russia, champion of the Slav people; he married an Italian princess of redoubtable Hapsburg lineage, and on the birth of his son Boris in 1893 he had the child baptized a Catholic, as if to emphasize the new Bulgarian state's independence of Orthodoxy.

But in 1894 Ferdinand set off one of those shifts in foreign policy for which his rule was to become famous, or notorious. He dismissed his dominating Prime Minister, Stefan Stambulov, who was murdered eighteen months later. Russo-Bulgarian relations now underwent a remarkable improvement; the infant heir to the throne, Boris, became a convert to the Orthodox faith, and in 1896 Tsar Nicholas II recognized Ferdinand as ruler of Bulgaria. Since the principality was still technically under Turkish suzerainty, Bulgarian foreign policy aimed at complete independence, and Ferdinand set up pro-Russian or pro-Austrian administrations depending on the prevailing attitude of Vienna and St Petersburg towards the Turkish Empire. At last in 1908 Austria, which needed Bulgarian support for its annexation of Bosnia-Herzegovina, offered Sofia the more solid diplomatic backing against Constantinople and Ferdinand made haste to proclaim his country's independence and himself as 'Tsar of All the Bulgarias'.

Tsar Ferdinand, though enjoying a well-nigh autocratic position, almost came to grief during the fierce and highly complex Balkan Wars of 1912–13. As a result of the First Balkan War of 1912, four Balkan powers (Bulgaria, Serbia, Montenegro and Greece) made substantial territorial gains from Turkey. But the Bulgarians and the Greeks and the Serbs quarrelled over the sharing out of Macedonia with its Aegean coastline. In Sofia the powerful International Macedonian Revolutionary Organization, and army leaders, turned on Ferdinand and presented him with a virtual ultimatum: there would be a military coup unless the advance into Macedonia was resumed. Ferdinand gave way, and in June 1913 Bulgaria launched a surprise attack on her former allies. The Bulgarians were worsted in the fighting and had to accept in settlement a valley in Macedonia, a strip of eastern Thrace and a second-rate Aegean port at Dedeagatch.

The general dissatisfaction in Bulgaria with the outcome of the Balkan Wars was responsible for the country's alliance with the Central Powers during the First World War. The Kaiser, Wilhelm II, personally distrusted Ferdinand, and had earlier rebuffed proposals for an alliance, but by 1915 Bulgaria had thrown in its lot with Germany, Austria and Turkey. The war went badly for the Bulgarians, especially due to Greek successes on the Salonica front, and in September 1918 a republic was proclaimed in the small manufacturing town of Radomir with the peasant leader Stamboliisky as president. A brief civil war ensued, which the old order won; republicanism evaporated with the general peace, and the monarchy was finally saved by Ferdinand's abdication in favour of his son, Boris III.

The new Bulgarian Tsar was soon faced with the remarkable phenomenon of Stamboliisky's premiership from 1919 to 1923: the peasant leader relied for support on the powerful Agrarian Party and was considered to be 'soft' on Bulgaria's Communists. When in April 1923 the Agrarian Party won 212 of the 245 seats in the Sobranjie, Stamboliisky began to urge the holding of a referendum on the future of the monarchy. This sealed his fate; Boris and the army launched a coup, during which Stamboliisky was captured and murdered. A Communist rising in September was crushed with calculated cruelty. By the end of 1923 probably 10,000 Bulgarians had been killed in the disturbances, and power now rested firmly with Boris and the army which was represented by Colonel Volkov. Peasant rule had been swept aside, and its place was taken by unbridled military dictatorship.

By 1936 Boris had dispensed with all but the forms of parliamentary government; though elections were held to the reconstituted Sobranjie in 1938 and married women allowed to vote for the first time, the results were of little importance since all the old parties were banned and the Sobranjie was merely a consultative body. Boris was dictator in all but name, but by no means unpopular with his people.

Though there could be no doubt of Boris's sympathies towards fascism, and though Bulgaria entered the Second World War as an ally of the Axis Powers, the country was not a slavish satellite of Nazi Germany. Boris prudently declined to send troops to assist the German invasion of Russia, and in 1943, after the collapse of Italy and amid the growing threat to the New Order in Europe, Boris was summoned before Hitler at Schloss Klessheim, near Salzburg, and angrily told that his country's fate depended on a total German victory; Boris appears to have been unperturbed, and gave the Führer as good as he got.

Perhaps because Bulgaria had so far done well out of the war, Boris remained a popular monarch, walking openly through the streets of Sofia – which was appropriate enough for a great-grandson of France's 'citizen King' Louis Philippe. On 28 August 1943, however, Boris died suddenly, immediately after returning from a visit to Hitler at his East Prussian headquarters. Foul play was suspected, but unproven. A Council of Regency was set up under Boris's brother Prince Cyril for the six-year-old heir Simeon.

Simeon II's reign was short-lived. In the wake of the Russian invasion of Bulgaria, the populist Fatherland Front won the election of 1945. A purge removed Prince Cyril and other leading monarchists. In 1946 a referendum showed that ninety-two per cent of the Bulgarian people wanted an end to the monarchy. Consequently the boy Tsar Simeon and his mother left the country, and on 15 September 1946 Bulgaria was proclaimed a People's Republic. Today ex-Tsar Simeon and his wife live apparently comfortable lives as part of the international jet-set, and are sometimes photographed at lavish parties for 'beautiful people'.

171 Tsar Ferdinand of Bulgaria (front, second from left) in 1914, on a visit to the Kaiser. Ferdinand became ruler of Bulgaria, then a newly united state, in 1887 and managed to remain Tsar until 1918, when he handed over to his son, Boris.

172 Like Albania, Bulgaria was fond of portraits depicting its rulers in idealized poses: the Bulgarian Queen displays her profile.

173 In the 1914–18 war, Bulgaria threw in her lot with Germany and Austria. The picture shows Ferdinand (making an observation) with his ally, Karl I of Austria (right) and Crown Prince Boris of Bulgaria, on the Austrian front.

174 Tsar Boris III, a tough but not unpopular dictator, and his wife.

175 (Above, opposite) Tsar Boris with his General Staff at a march-past in Sofia.

176 (Below, opposite) Boris III, in 1938, studying a map with his war minister, General Daskalov (left) during the autumn manoeuvres of the Bulgarian army. Boris was too independent an ally for Hitler's taste; he refused to send troops to invade Russia.

177 (Above left) Boris, on a visit to Belgrade, with Prince Paul, the Regent of Yugoslavia.

178 (Below left) Boris is bid farewell by Franz von Papen just after his visit to Hitler in August 1943. He died suddenly and mysteriously on his return and, though never proved, foul play was suspected.

179 (Above right) Boris with his Prime Minister, Kimeon Georgiev, in 1934. Georgiev was soon to be imprisoned.

180 (Below right) Tsar Simeon II of Bulgaria, Boris's son. He was only six when his father died, and when he was nine he was ousted by a referendum and left the country with his mother (in 1946). He married the Spanish heiress Margarita Gomez-Acero y Cejuela; the picture shows the couple on the occasion of their engagement.

Romania

Romania was declared a kingdom in 1881, its two constituent principalities of Moldavia and Wallachia having gained independence as a result of supporting Russia in the war against Turkey in 1877. Prince Carol of Hohenzollern-Sigmaringen was translated into King Carol I in 1881. Carol's dynastic connections with the German royal house were impeccable, and his reign, which lasted until his death in 1914, was a successful one. By prudently staying out of the First Balkan War and by entering the Second, Romania gained the southern Dobrudja region from Bulgaria.

King Carol's rule was hardly a model of modest constitutional monarchy. He continued to exercise considerable authority: he had the right of absolute veto over legislation, could appoint and dismiss ministers as he chose, and could dissolve parliaments as he saw fit. When in 1883 he negotiated a secret treaty of alliance with Germany and the Austrian Empire, he had no hesitation in locking it away in his private safe and (on the Romanian side), apart from himself, only his Prime Minister and Foreign Minister knew of the document's existence.

King Ferdinand succeeded his father to the throne in 1914. His Queen was a grand-daughter of Queen Victoria and the daughter of Alfred, Duke of Edinburgh, the old queen's second son. Marie of Edinburgh, who was known to the family as 'Missy', was clever, conceited and melodramatic. Not only did her marriage to Ferdinand ('Nando') link the Romanian royal family with the House of Windsor, but her daughter Princess Marie married King Alexander of Yugoslavia and her second daughter married King George II of Greece.

Romanian territory was spectacularly extended under King Ferdinand. The country was persuaded by the prospect of territorial gain to enter the First World War on the Allied side in 1916. By January 1917, however, most of the country had been occupied by Germany and Austria-Hungary, and the Romanians were forced to make a separate peace in March 1918. With the collapse of the Central Powers in the autumn of 1918 Romania hastily re-entered the war on 9 November, two days before the armistice. At the peace conferences Romania received all her promised territory, including Transylvania, Bessarabia and much of the Hungarian plain, thus more than doubling her size.

Between the wars Romania, for all its great wheat-fields and valuable oil wells, frittered away its economic opportunities so that the overall standard of living was actually lower in 1939 than in 1914. Much of the responsibility for Romania's unhappy history in the years between the two World Wars belongs to the royal family. King Ferdinand was only too eager to keep democracy (and hence Bolshevism) at bay. Under the new constitution of 1923 the crown retained its considerable powers, which in fact allowed it to override parliament; both the monarch and the corrupt Liberal party benefited from this constitution.

A further unpleasant phenomenon was the foundation of a Romanian fascist party, the Iron Guard, in 1923. Its begetter, Corneliu Codreanu, claimed that he had been granted a vision by the Archangel Michael, who had charged him with the task of leading the moral regeneration of Romania. The Iron Guard perpetrated violent attacks upon Jews and other minority groups, and was the only fascist movement in the Balkans to attract really solid mass support.

Four years before he died in 1927 Ferdinand had removed his son Carol from the succession; Carol's fall was due to his scandalous private life and in particular to his attachment to his Jewish mistress, Madame Lupescu. Carol had been forced to renounce the throne in favour of his son Michael, who was only six years old when his grandfather Ferdinand died. The Council of Regency, acting for Michael, was rash enough to allow free elections and a restoration of parliamentary government in 1928.

This new era lasted for two years. In 1930 the Prime Minister, Maniu, hoping to avoid a lengthy Regency, invited the exiled Carol back. Having privately undertaken to give up Madame Lupescu (a promise he had no intention of keeping) Carol flew to Bucharest on 6 June 1930 and dramatically claimed his throne. On 4 August Madame Lupescu slipped back into the country, and two months later Maniu resigned.

Democracy was now at an end. Political life came to be increasingly dominated by King Carol II; the monarch was little more than a seedy playboy, quite lacking in genuine statecraft. In February 1938 Carol set up a 'Cabinet of National Concentration', which was an extreme right-wing royalist government from which members of the Iron Guard (which the King distrusted as rivals) were excluded. Three weeks later Carol pushed through a new constitutional law that gave all essential powers to the monarch; political parties were suppressed, and the elections rigged to support the royal position.

Carol II fell from power in 1940 after he had surrendered vast territories to Axis and Soviet pressure: in eleven weeks he gave up Bessarabia and northern Bukovina (to Russia), two-fifths of Transylvania (to Hungary) and the southern Dobrudja (to Bulgaria). Thus the dictates of the German-Russian pact of 1939 and the demands of the Nazis' eastern European sympathizers were satisfied. The Romanian people, however, were not satisfied; the Iron Guard whipped up discontent, and on 6 September 1940 Carol abdicated in favour of his son Michael and fled into exile.

General Ion Antonescu now became the real ruler of the country and a puppet of Hitler. Vile pogroms and political murders became commonplace. In 1941 German troops were sent in to support Antonescu against the fanatics of the Iron Guard; the Guard was destroyed, and Antonescu became the nation's 'Conducator' (the equivalent of Führer or Duce); the kingdom was now clearly controlled by the 'Conducator', the army and the Germans.

Though Romania participated enthusiastically in Hitler's invasion of Russia, and suffered heavy losses, the balance of war gradually tilted against her. In 1944, with the Red Army driving westwards, King Michael had Antonescu and the latter's son arrested and detained in a ventilated safe used by ex-King Carol II for the royal stamp collection. The next day (24 August) Romania changed sides, as Italy had done earlier. King Michael received widespread praise and the Soviet 'Order of Victory' for his coup, but within two and a half years his position had been rendered intolerable by Communist political success.

He clung grimly to his throne, however, and in 1947 went to London to attend the wedding of his cousin Princess Elizabeth. While absent from his country he became engaged to Princess Anne of Bourbon-Parma, but on his return to Bucharest he found that the Democratic National Front government did not approve of a royal wedding and demanded his abdication instead. On 30 December 1947 he signed a document of abdication and went into exile, as popular as ever; he was later to protest that he had abdicated under duress, and that the action therefore lacked validity. In 1948 Romania was declared a People's Republic. Ex-King Michael today lives in Switzerland, and regularly visits his Windsor cousins in Britain.

181 (Opposite) The bizarre poetess-queen, Elizabeth of Romania, who wrote under the name of Carmen Sylva, with her husband King Carol I.

182 (Above left) Queen Marie of Romania, Queen Victoria's grand-daughter 'Missy'; beautiful, clever, conceited, she loved dressing up; here she wears Romanian peasant costume to place flowers on her son's grave.

183 (Right) Marie greeting grizzled war veterans during the anniversary celebrations of the union of the Dobrudja with Romania. This was the sort of ceremony she loved and carried out superbly.

184 (Below) Queen Marie in the exotic setting that she contrived for herself in the Cotroceni palace. Shades of 'Elinor Glyn on tiger skin'!

S.D. Prinz Karl v. Hohenzollern

185 (Above left, opposite) King Carol I (standing) having his cap adjusted by his cigar-smoking younger brother, Prince Carl of Hohenzollern. His elder brother, Prince Wilhelm, is seated with the ladies; Marie appears to be holding a cigarette in her right hand.

186 (Below left, opposite) A hunting party in 1936, organized by Queen Marie of Yugoslavia, daughter of Marie of Romania, to entertain her brother, Carol II of Romania, and his son Crown Prince Michael. King Carol is to the right of Queen Marie of Yugoslavia's bulky figure; Prince Michael to the left.

187 (Left) Carol II of Romania. He was the centre of many scandals; his father, King Ferdinand, said of him on his deathbed, 'Carol is like a Swiss cheese, excellent for what it is, but so full of holes'.

188 (Right) Madame Elena Lupescu, Carol's divorced, Jewish mistress, for whom he renounced his right to the throne in 1925, leaving his wife, Helen of Greece.

189 (Left) General Antonescu, Romania's strongarm ruler during the war years. He was arrested on King Michael's orders in 1944.

190 (Below) King Ferdinand and Queen Marie on a visit to Athens.

191 (Above, opposite) The son of Carol II and Helen of Greece, King Michael, who twice ascended the Romanian throne. The first time was as a boy of five on the death of his grandfather Ferdinand in 1927. His father Carol was then reinstated in 1930. Prince Michael succeeded to the throne for the second time when Carol abdicated and went into exile in 1940.

   The picture shows Michael (left) with the Russian General Susiakov at a 1946 military parade in Bucharest to celebrate Romania's break-away from Germany at the end of the Second World War.

192 (a) (Below, opposite) King Michael of Romania in more carefree days.

192 (b) King Michael in exile in 1951 with his wife, Princess Anne of Bourbon, on a visit to London.

Yugoslavia

The Kingdom of Yugoslavia was created by the peace treaties of 1919, though it was officially called the 'Serb-Croat-Slovene Kingdom' until 1929. The King of Serbia was elevated to the throne of Yugoslavia as Peter I, after King Nicholas of Montenegro had been conveniently deposed. Peter had become King of Serbia in 1903 in tragic circumstances. The former King, Alexander Obrenovič, had alienated the General Staff and the powerful Radical Party by marrying his mistress, Draga Mašin, in 1900. A campaign of vilification was launched against the dynasty and in May 1903 officers of the Belgrade garrison broke into the royal palace and shot down the King and Queen before throwing the naked corpses into the garden; some ministers and relatives of the Queen were also killed.

The assassinations caused Edward VII to withdraw British recognition of the Serbian government, and the Russian foreign minister proposed that Austrian troops should be sent to restore order in Belgrade. The Serbs provided their own solution, however, by inviting the seventy-year-old Peter Karadjordjevič (a relative of the murdered King) to accept the crown. Peter was a good choice: he believed in constitutional government, he had a fine military reputation, and it was even said he supported the ideal of South Slav unity.

A short while before the assassination of the Archduke Ferdinand at Sarajevo in June 1914, King Peter had made way for his son, the Crown Prince Alexander, to act as Regent on his behalf. The First World War, which followed almost immediately, provided the melting-pot out of which emerged the new Kingdom of Yugoslavia. Since the aged King Peter was still alive he became titular monarch of the new state, with Alexander continuing as Prince-Regent. In 1921, on his father's death, Alexander became King in his own right.

Alexander married Princess Marie of Romania, a great-grand-daughter of Queen Victoria; in 1923 the Duke of York (the future King George VI) went to Belgrade to act as 'Koom' (Godfather) to the couple's infant son (the future King Peter of Yugoslavia). The Duke of York played an heroic role during the christening, rescuing the Crown Prince from the font where the Patriarch had dropped him, carrying his screaming godson on a cushion throughout the ceremony, and receiving, unabashed, a present of a set of hand-embroidered underwear.

King Alexander had the high intention of behaving as a constitutional monarch and serving as a trustee for all his people. However his training as a soldier inclined him to see dissent as mutiny; he thus tended to favour the Slovenes at the expense of the Croats. In June 1928 a Montenegrin deputy in the Yugoslav parliament shot two Croatian Peasant members dead and wounded three others. Alexander was appalled at these events and desperately sought a solution to the tensions within his country.

Eventually in January 1929 Alexander decided to take over himself; he dismantled the 1921 constitution, dissolved the existing political parties, muzzled the press, and shared executive power with a council of ministers. This royal dictatorship was plainly anti-democratic, though not, at the outset, unpopular. But the brutalities of the Yugoslavian police, the persecution of the Communists and the Peasant Party, and the plight of Croatia ensured that those who had sowed the wind (notably the King) would reap the whirlwind.

In 1934 King Alexander was murdered in Marseilles shortly after he had begun a State visit to France; the French Foreign Minister, Louis Barthou, died with him. Alexander was gunned down by a member of the International Macedonian Revolutionary Organization who was one of a group of Croatian terrorists who had been harboured in Hungary and who had hatched their plot in Italy. The dead King had been flirting with the new Nazi regime in Germany, and he had been invited to France chiefly to ensure that he would support the French diplomatic position rather than the German.

Alexander's crown passed to his eleven-year-old son Peter. But a Regency was necessary until Peter should reach the age of eighteen; the chief Regent was Alexander's cousin, Prince Paul. The Regent privately deplored Alexander's militaristic dictatorship, and was no partisan of Serbia as the dead King had been. If he had succeeded to the Yugoslav throne, Paul might have done a great deal to restore democracy and reconcile the regional rivalries of the state. As it was he did his best to improve Yugoslavia's relations with her neighbours; he found Marshal Goering a congenial man to deal with, but came to distrust the ambitions of Mussolini's Italy. In 1939 Paul did, in fact, grant Croatia a substantial degree of autonomy, but failed to democratize the constitution for fear of invasion by Yugoslavia's Axis neighbours.

When the Second World War broke out, Paul's Regency still had two years to run. Britain and America urged him to stand firm against Hitler, and he received personal messages from Winston Churchill, Roosevelt and George VI encouraging him to keep out of the Axis camp. But the pressures to declare some degree of support for Germany were immense, and, as Paul reminded the American ambassador, 'You big nations are hard. You talk of honour but you are far away.' In March 1941 the Yugoslavian government signed a pact of alliance with Germany. Within days units of the Yugoslavian army and air force, encouraged by British agents and the British government, swept away Paul's Regency in a lightning coup.

A little more than a week later German dive-bombers struck at Belgrade, and a joint German, Italian, Hungarian and Bulgarian force invaded Yugoslavia. The Croats turned upon the Serbs and were rewarded by Hitler with the status of an independent kingdom ruled (*in absentia*) by the Italian Duke of Spoleto. Yugoslavia was partitioned: torn to shreds as a national unit.

The young King, Peter II, fought bravely with his armies, then fled. He soon left his government-in-exile to bicker in Cairo and went on to study (appropriately enough) International Law at Cambridge University. As the Yugoslav partisans, led by Josip Tito, fought back heroically against the Axis powers, so King Peter's prospects of restoration waned. By the end of 1945 the Communist Party was in a dominant position, and in November of that year the newly elected Parliament proclaimed Yugoslavia a 'Federal People's Republic'. The throne of King Peter had collapsed, like so many of his Balkan equivalents, under the blows of war and the pressures of the peace. The deposed monarch went into exile in the United States, where he died several years ago.

193 King Alexander I of Serbia (later Yugoslavia). He and his wife, formerly his mistress Draga Mašin, were murdered by Serbian officers in Belgrade, 1903.

194 (Below left) Peter I of Serbia, who in 1903 succeeded the murdered Alexander I, riding through the streets of Belgrade at his coronation.

195 (Below right) A paunchy King Nicholas of Montenegro with his daughter, the Queen of Italy. Montenegro was later absorbed into the new Yugoslavia, Nicholas having been deposed.

196 (Above, opposite) The christening of Crown Prince Peter of Yugoslavia in 1923. Queen Marie of Romania, resplendent in a pearl tiara, holds her grandson on her knee. The others are, left to right: King Alexander of Yugoslavia (father), the Queen of Greece (aunt), King Ferdinand of Romania (grandfather), the Duchess of York and the Duke of York, later Britain's King George VI (godfather).

197 (Below, opposite) The marriage of King Alexander I of Yugoslavia to Princess Marie of Romania. Queen Marie of Romania, wearing drop earrings, is the central figure; her daughter, the bride, sits between her mother and her husband.

198 (Left) King Alexander of Yugoslavia with the eldest of his three sons, later King Peter II.

199 (Below) King Alexander and Queen Marie at the railway station in Belgrade. They were an unaffected, calm and practical pair, imperturbable under the constant threat of assassination.

200 Prince Paul of Yugoslavia (left), King Alexander's cousin and close friend. He took over as Regent after Alexander's assassination in 1934. This photograph was taken in 1936 and shows him deep in conversation with his Prime Minister, Stoyadinovich.

201 *King Alexander of Yugoslavia and Louis Barthou lying in state in Marseilles after their assassination.*

202 *The bloodstained interior of the open car in which Alexander was being driven through the streets of Marseilles with the French Foreign Minister, Louis Barthou. A Croatian terrorist, Velucko Kerin, leaped on to the running board and shot Alexander and Barthou dead, wounding the third person in the car, General Georges, who later recovered. Kerin himself was badly injured and died a few hours later.*

203 *(Above right) A group of the Croatian terrorists who finally succeeded in their attempts to assassinate Alexander. The second man from the left is said to be the assassin himself.*

204 *(Below right) Prince Paul of Yugoslavia during his Regency (1934–1941) on behalf of the young King Peter II.*

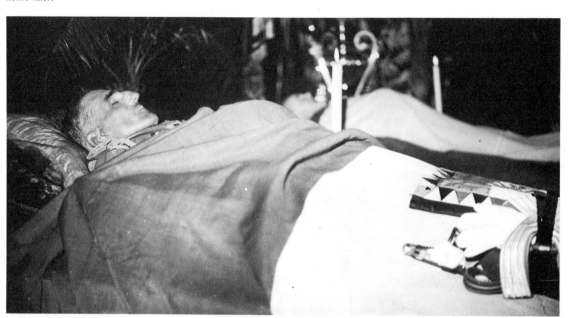

205 *King Peter II of Yugoslavia in 1937, on holiday at a boys' camp on the shore of Lake Bled. He appears to be trying to impose his will on reluctant comrades.*

206 *Hitler, after his attack on Yugoslavia in 1941, pronounced Croatia an independent country. He appointed the Italian Duke of Spoleto, pictured here, as the King of Croatia, but the Duke never dared to enter his kingdom.*

207 *After the assassination of Alexander, Queen Marie spent much time in England, where her two younger sons were at school. This family photograph was taken on one of her summer visits to Yugoslavia. In the back row are King Peter and Queen Marie on the left; Prince Paul (the Regent) his wife and family on the right.*

208 *Crown Prince Alexander of Yugoslavia. In 1970, after the death of his father, King Peter, the Prince – a naturalized British citizen – turned down a suggestion that he should be crowned in exile.*

*209 King Peter at a Serbian orthodox Christmas celebration
in London, 1951.*

*210 (Below) Prince Paul of Yugoslavia in 1962, with
Princess Maria Pia at a funeral in Paris.*

Greece

As the twentieth century opened, King George I of the Hellenes had been the monarch since his unanimous election in 1864. He was the second son of the late King of Denmark and hence brother-in-law to Britain's Edward VII, as well as a beloved uncle of the future King George V, with whom he had earlier exchanged warm letters including such appetising endearments as 'my dear old sausage' and 'my dear old pickled pork'.

Under George I (1864–1913) Greece enjoyed a democratic constitution in which the powers of the monarch, though considerably more substantial than the shadowy prerogatives of the British crown, were strictly defined. Greek democracy also owed something to the ethnic and religious homogeneity of the Greek state.

But the possibility of strong-arm action by the military, who felt entitled to intervene in political affairs, was never far away. In 1909 a militant organization, the Military League, forced the government's resignation and obliged the King to accept the dismissal of all his sons from their service posts. After more than a year the Military League agreed to its own dissolution and summoned Venizelos to become Prime Minister. Under the resulting constitutional amendments of 1911 the Council of State was revived as a Crown Council, the quorum for the elected Chamber was reduced, officers were declared ineligible for election, civil servants were guaranteed security of tenure, free, compulsory education introduced, and a new military post created for Crown Prince Constantine who had been so abruptly dismissed two years before. The new constitution left the monarch's powers much as they were before; the changes were, for the most part, practical adjustments to the experience of the previous decades.

On 18 March 1913 King George was assassinated by a madman in Salonika; in his fifty years' reign he had established an enviable reputation for constitutional government. He also died in the interval between the Balkan Wars, from which Greece was to emerge with the valuable prizes of southern Epirus and Macedonia, as well as the islands of Crete and Samos – thus almost doubling the country's size. The new King, Constantine I, had played a distinguished part as Commander-in-Chief during the Balkan Wars and he therefore succeeded to the throne amid considerable popularity. Almost immediately, however, he was caught up in the diplomatic temptations and dangers of the First World War.

During the war Greece was bitterly divided between pro-Allied and pro-German factions. Constantine, who was married to Princess Sophie of Hohenzollern and was hence a brother-in-law of the Kaiser, was inclined to align Greece with Germany in the hope of fending off Bulgarian aggression aimed at recouping losses incurred during the Balkan Wars. But Venizelos was pro-British; the King broke with him, employed questionable constitutional tactics, and eventually saw the Allies recognize Venizelos's provisional government. In 1917 Constantine was ousted, and his second son succeeded him as King Alexander I; Greece was now fully committed to the Allied cause.

The Treaty of Sèvres was signed in 1920 and Greece's rewards in terms of territory were staggeringly generous; the treaty was never ratified, however, and the militant, revived Turkey of Kemal Ataturk was able eventually to thwart Greek ambitions. On 25 October King Alexander died suddenly after being bitten by a monkey; three weeks later Venizelos was heavily defeated in the general election, and in December a plebiscite resulted in an overwhelming majority in favour of Constantine's restoration.

But in September 1922, following the massive Turkish triumph at Smyrna, Constantine abdicated and retired to Sicily where he died four months later. The Crown Prince now ascended the throne as George II; his inheritance was one of indescribable chaos and in the December 1923 elections the Republicans, strongly backed by the High Command of the armed forces, won over one-third of the seats. In January 1924 King George agreed to leave the country for three months while the constitutional problem was settled. On 25 March, however, a republic was declared, though the King had not abdicated; a subsequent plebiscite showed that one-third of the electorate were monarchist.

After eleven uneasy years the republic faded away, aided by General Kondylis, the Minister for War; on 3 November 1935 a plebiscite (widely suspected of having been manipulated by the army) produced a vote of 97 per cent in favour of King George II's restoration, and by the end of the month the monarch was back in Athens. King George became more and more dependent upon his dictatorial Prime Minister, General Metaxas, who supervised a policy of semi-fascist authoritarianism; left-wing political parties were crushed, the secret police were active, and the constitution was suspended. But the regime, though right-wing, was determined to retain the nation's integrity even against Italy and Germany. Mussolini's invasion of 1940 was beaten back, but this only encouraged Hitler to come to his blundering ally's support early in 1941. Until October 1944, when British troops finally liberated Athens, both Communist and monarchist guerrilla groups fought against the Axis occupation.

Once the Axis threat was removed Greece was plunged into a bitter civil war which lasted until 1949. In 1947 King George II had died and was succeeded by his younger brother Paul, who finally managed to assert the position of the monarchy. King Paul's reign, which lasted until 1964, was tarnished by accusations of right-wing leanings. His Queen, Frederika (a former German princess), was reputedly an autocrat and was also suspected of mishandling a royal fund raised during the civil war for the relief of refugees. Republicans pointed to royal extravagance amid widespread economic hardship.

When King Paul died of cancer in 1964 the crown passed to his handsome, twenty-three-year-old son, Constantine. King Constantine II had won a gold medal at the 1960 Olympic Games as a yachtsman; he was also engaged to the beautiful Princess Anne-Marie of Denmark. Though hopes were high at the outset of Constantine's reign, the 'Colonels' coup' in 1967 brought extreme authoritarian government back to Greece. On 13 December 1967 Constantine, who had earlier endorsed the coup, tried to overthrow his military masters by rallying loyalist support; the army failed to respond, and within twenty-four hours the King fled to Rome accompanied by his family.

Like so many throne-less monarchs before him, Constantine eventually made his way to Britain. At first the Colonels claimed that he had 'voluntarily abstained' from his duties, and was welcome to return at any time. Constantine chose not to pay the price of his return – the abandonment of his constitutional powers. In July 1974 the Colonels were ousted and democratic government restored. The monarchy, however, was not restored, and in a referendum later in the year the result (on a 76 per cent turnout) showed 69 per cent opposed to the King's restoration and 31 per cent for it. Given the turbulence of recent Greek history, however, it is by no means impossible that one day Constantine will return to his uneasy inheritance.

211 *A romantic picture of the Danish prince, who became George of Greece. He was a brother of Queen Alexandra of England and of the Empress Marie of Russia, and was elected King of the Hellenes at the age of 19. George reigned as a constitutional monarch for nearly fifty years; in 1913 he was assassinated by a madman.*

212 *(Centre) George's son, King Constantine of Greece, who had two periods of rule in his chequered life; 1913–17 and 1920–22.*

213 *(Above right) King Constantine was a successful soldier and Commander-in-Chief in the Balkan wars. Here, in white uniform, he confers with his General Staff at the front.*

214 *(Below right) Constantine with his family. His wife, Queen Sophie, was the Kaiser's sister; this, coupled with Constantine's efforts to remain neutral in the 1914–18 war, led to the Greek royal family being considered pro-German. In fact Sophie thought her brother rather absurd and tended to identify herself with the English cause.*

215 George II of Greece with President Roosevelt during the Second World War. He was the son of Constantine and Sophie, and came to the throne when his father finally abdicated in 1922. In 1924 he left Greece, but was recalled as the result of a plebiscite in 1935, after which he ruled until Hitler invaded Greece in 1941.

216 (Below) King George II's younger brother and successor, King Paul, on a visit to Madrid in 1963. He was photographed in the Prado Palace sharing a joke with General Franco.

217 (Right) King Paul in Salonika in 1960, kissing the Holy Gospel held by the Archbishop of Salonika.

218 (Left) King Paul's wife, the unpopular and allegedly arch-reactionary Queen Frederika.

219 An adolescent Crown Prince Constantine, King Paul's son, talking to Elizabeth Taylor at a film première in Athens in 1958.

220 (Below) A year earlier he had himself been an actor: in a production of a Sophoclean tragedy at Anavrtya College.

221 *Britain's Prince Charles and Princess Anne, windswept at Athens airport, with their grandmother, Princess Alice of Greece. They had come to attend King Constantine's marriage to Princess Anne Marie of Denmark in 1964, the year in which Constantine had succeeded to the throne.*

222 *(Centre) Princess Alice (Princess Andrew) of Greece, the daughter of Prince Louis of Battenberg, the sister of Lord Mountbatten of Burma and the mother of the Duke of Edinburgh. She lived in England for many years until her*

death in 1972; links between Greek and British royal families are therefore strong and ex-King Constantine has settled in England with his family.

223 *(Right) Hopes were high for the attractive young King and his bride in 1964: Constantine and Anne Marie at their wedding reception at the Royal Palace.*

Chapter Six

The Low Countries

The Netherlands

The Dutch monarchy dates only from 1814 when Holland, Belgium and Luxemburg were united under King William of Orange-Nassau. In 1830, however, the Belgians proclaimed their independence, and in 1890 Luxemburg became an independent Grand Duchy on the accession of Queen Wilhelmina – for tradition would not allow a woman to become the province's ruler.

Rather than progressing, as so many states have, from monarchy to republic, the Dutch enjoyed centuries of robust republicanism before accepting a fully-fledged monarchy. But the first monarch of the new kingdom came from the illustrious House of Orange which had previously succeeded in making the Stadtholdership of the Dutch Republic hereditary. The transition from republic to monarchy was therefore lacking in profound drama or in trauma, since, in a sense, the position of King was merely an extension of the office of Stadtholder.

Oddly, the Dutch have been ruled by women ever since 1890, when William III died and Queen Emma acted as regent for the child-queen Wilhelmina. Ascending the throne in 1898 Queen Wilhelmina reigned for fifty years before abdicating in favour of her daughter Juliana in 1948. During the greater part of Wilhelmina's reign the Dutch enjoyed peace and prosperity; the nation remained neutral during the First World War and, until the Japanese conquests in the Far East during the Second World War, boasted a substantial overseas empire in Indonesia (as well as in the Caribbean). When the Germans invaded the Netherlands in 1940 the royal family fled to Britain, from which refuge Queen Wilhelmina made regular and defiant broadcasts to her occupied kingdom. After her abdication she retired to her palace Het Loo and devoted herself to writing her memoirs and to religious study; she insisted on being known as Princess Wilhelmina; she died, aged eighty-two, in 1962.

Queen Juliana married Prince Bernhard, Prince of Lippe-Biesterfeld, in 1937, after the latter had left his native Germany following Hitler's rise to power. The royal couple had four children – all daughters. The Queen's reign has been marked by a number of controversies. In 1956 foreign newspapers published stories that Queen Juliana had consulted a faith-healer (reputed to be a female equivalent of Rasputin) to help cure her youngest daughter Princess Christina of her blindness; there were further reports of a constitutional crisis and of a rift between the Queen and her husband over the whole affair. Eventually a three-man commission stated that Princess Christina was not blind, but had a clouding of her eyes; it was also stated that the Queen had severed all connections with the faith-healer and that there had been no real danger of her abdicating. Many Dutch observers blamed the foreign press for inflating what was essentially a private matter.

More significant was the 1964 controversy over the engagement of Princess Irene, then second in succession to the throne, to Prince Carlos Hugo of Bourbon-Parma, son of the Carlist pretender to the Spanish throne. Princess Irene became a Catholic prior to her marriage. Even though the Dutch constitution does not stipulate that the monarch must be a Protestant, each monarch has in fact been a member of the Dutch Reformed Church. Moreover the House of Orange had been closely identified with the Netherlands' rebellion against the Catholic Spain of King Philip II in the late sixteenth century. Princess Irene's marriage thus raised the ancient spectre of Spain and Rome in ominous alliance. Still, Princess Irene did marry Prince Carlos Hugo, even though she renounced her right of succession and undertook to live outside the Netherlands.

A year later a more bitter controversy arose over Queen Juliana's announcement that her eldest daughter, the Crown Princess Beatrix, was going to marry a German diplomat, Claus von Amsberg. Since Princess Beatrix was next in line to the throne the choice of her husband was a particularly delicate one; yet von Amsberg was a German who had served in the Wehrmacht during the Second World War and had previously belonged to the Hitler Youth movement. The German occupation of the Netherlands had left many unpleasant memories, and Jews, former resistance members and socialists protested against the proposed marriage. Although the engaged couple won considerable support after a relaxed and frank press conference, their wedding occasioned some violence. The wedding was held in Amsterdam (thus breaking the tradition that the monarch is married at The Hague, inaugurated in Amsterdam and buried at Delft) in March 1966, after a government bill approving the marriage had passed parliament by 132 votes to 9. Orange swastikas were painted on the walls of the royal palace in Amsterdam, and during the wedding procession fireworks and smokebombs were thrown; nineteen arrests were made, and half of Amsterdam's municipal councillors refused to attend the wedding. Despite his mixed reception, Claus von Amsberg (now Prince Claus) has fathered three royal sons: Willem Alexander, born in 1967; Johan Friso, born in 1968; and Constantijn, born in 1969. At the very least, therefore, the marriage of Crown Princess Beatrix has assured that one day the Netherlands will have a King once more.

The Dutch monarchy is a popular institution nationally, many people judging it to be a unifying factor. In an opinion poll published in 1969 by the weekly review *Elseviers Week Blad* only 10 per cent of those questioned wanted a republic, while 70 per cent were satisfied with the way the Queen did her job. Doubtless the democratic deportment of the royal family has something to do with this. The Dutch monarch is no longer crowned, merely inaugurated at a simple ceremony attended by both houses of parliament; Queen Juliana lives at Soestdijk Palace, some twenty miles from Amsterdam – a modest white-painted building, with its lawns open to public view from the road. Princess Beatrix lives at a small palace near her mother. When they were growing up the four princesses cycled to school each day: to New Baarn primary and Baarn grammar school. Queen Juliana also cycles, as did her mother before her; she also buys at least some of her clothes ready-made. Just as in Britain Prince Philip has received a good deal of the credit for the more relaxed bearing of the House of Windsor, so in the Netherlands Prince Bernhard has played an equivalent role.

Queen Juliana is, however, a rich woman. She has a large private fortune and receives a salary of some 850,000 guilders (approximately £135,000) from the state which also pays most of the expense of royal households, official receptions, state visits and the like. Although the Queen is rumoured to be the richest woman in the world, she is probably not even the richest woman in the Netherlands.

Constitutionally the Dutch monarch is titular president of the Council of State which sees all Bills before they are presented to parliament and also acts as the highest court of appeal in administrative cases. Also, after general elections, the monarch consults the chairmen of both houses of parliament, party leaders and the vice-president of the Council of State; if an obvious leader has emerged the Queen will appoint him *formateur* of a government; if no such leader is apparent she will appoint a *formateur* (often an appropriate elder statesman) to sound out opinion and see if a government can be formed. All parliamentary bills have to receive the royal assent. Despite these constitutional powers, the Dutch monarchy is moving very much with the times, and by so doing will doubtless maintain itself as a fulcrum of national unity.

225 *The Dutch style of monarchy is now informal and democratic; Queen Juliana and her retinue, led by the local* burgomasters, *cycling through Friesland after the Queen had opened a water-purifying plant in the area.*

226 *The young Wilhelmina in Dutch peasant costume.*

227 *(Below left) Queen Wilhelmina as a girl of 19; she had been on the throne for a year, following the regency of her mother, Queen Emma, from 1890 to 1898.*

228 *(Above right) Wilhelmina's father, King William III, who died in 1890. Since that date, the Dutch have been ruled by women.*

229 *(Below right) Queen Emma of the Netherlands.*

230 *(Above, opposite) Queen Wilhelmina, driving with the King of the Belgians. At this stage, Holland was still an imperial power with large possessions in Indonesia and the Caribbean, and the royal family was very far from the informality of today.*

231 *(Below, opposite) Queen Juliana of the Netherlands with George VI on a state visit to London, November 1950.*

232 *Juliana as a girl of 13, with her Maids of Honour in the Flemish costumes presented to her on her 13th birthday by the burgomaster of Middelburg. The women of Middelburg still wear their traditional costume today.*

234 *(Right) Queen Juliana of the Netherlands, with her husband Prince Bernhard, whom she married in 1937, and the first of their four daughters.*

233 *(Below) Queen Wilhelmina fled from Holland with her family from the German invasion in 1940. In exile, she did what she could to help her occupied country, broadcasting frequently to her people. This picture shows her broadcasting in America during the war, campaigning on Holland's behalf.*

235 *Juliana (second from left) on a visit to New York. The others are Crown Prince Olaf of Norway, Mrs Roosevelt (holding a glass), and Crown Princess Martha of Norway.*

236 *(Below) Queen Juliana and Prince Bernhard in 1950, with their four daughters, at their home, the unpretentious Soestdijk Palace in Utrecht, about 20 miles outside Amsterdam.*

237 *(Right) Prince Bernhard at La Scala in Milan in 1958, talking to Birgit Nilson, the Swedish soprano, after a performance of Puccini's* Turandot.

238 Prince Bernhard is given the credit for much of the more relaxed atmosphere which now surrounds the Dutch royal family. Here he is at the controls of a new hovercraft in Amsterdam harbour, 1963.

239 (Below) Prince Bernhard, like the Duke of Edinburgh, has been involved with the preservation of wild life. This 1970 photograph shows Queen Juliana and Prince Bernhard arriving at a dinner in London on behalf of the World Wildlife Fund; Queen Juliana, rather oddly, wearing red fox furs. Peter Scott diplomatically said, 'It is fairly all right to wear ranched mink or fox. It is only slightly anti-wild life because these species are in no danger of extinction.'

240 (Above right) Crown Princess Beatrix of the Netherlands in 1966, ski-ing with her fiancé, Claus von Amsberg. The marriage in 1966 was unpopular as von Amsberg was a German who served in the Wehrmacht during World War II, and had belonged to the Hitler Youth movement.

241 (Below right) In 1964 Princess Irene, second daughter of Queen Juliana, became a Catholic and married Prince Carlos Hugo of Bourbon-Parma, son of the Carlist pretender to the Spanish throne. Princess Irene has renounced her rights of succession and has undertaken to live outside the Netherlands; here she and her husband have an audience with the Catholic Primate of Spain.

Belgium

The Belgian monarchy, founded in 1831, excludes women from the succession. Executive power is vested in the King, who can dissolve or prorogue parliament, appoint ministers and judges, make war and peace, issue currency, and confer titles and decorations; the King is also commander of the armed forces. The constitution, however, maintains that no act of the King is effective unless counter-signed by an appropriate minister, and that the monarch has no other powers beyond those allotted in the constitution.

But Belgium's earlier Kings established the tradition of an influential monarchy. King Leopold I (1831–65) exercised considerable influence over diplomatic and military decisions, and also began the tradition of presiding over cabinet meetings. His son Leopold II (1865–1909) interfered chronically in state affairs, and even set up his own notorious private empire in the Congo. By the time Albert I succeeded to the throne in 1909 the monarchy's popularity was badly shaken, and his more constitutional deportment was needed to restore it. King Albert played an active part in affairs of state, but strictly within the constitution, and he only rarely presided over cabinet meetings – though he did so more frequently during the crisis-ridden years of the First World War when much of Belgium was occupied and the government carried on in the remaining fragment of territory.

King Albert died in 1934 and was succeeded by his son, Leopold III. In 1940 the new King came close to destroying the Belgian monarchy by his order to his troops to capitulate and by his decision to remain a prisoner of the invading Germans rather than to follow his government into exile. The Belgian government-in-exile eventually declared Leopold's brother Charles to be regent, and in July 1945 the Belgian parliament passed a law making Leopold's return dependent on its own consent. Between 1945 and 1950 Leopold remained in exile, while successive cabinets tried to obtain assurances that he would never again defy ministerial advice as in 1940. Eventually a referendum was held in March 1950, as a result of which 51 per cent voted 'Yes' to the question 'Are you of the opinion that King Leopold III should resume the exercise of his constitutional powers?'

At the end of July 1950 a joint session of both houses of parliament voted for the King's return, but the majority was only a decisive one because the socialist members withdrew from the debate. On 22 July King Leopold flew back to Belgium accompanied by his two sons, Prince Baudouin and Prince Albert. Immediately the nation was disrupted by strikes and protests, and at a meeting near Liège three men were shot dead by police. It was announced that 100,000 strikers would march on Brussels on 1 August, and road blocks were set up round the city. Desperate all-party talks took place on 31 July and continued until 6.30 a.m. on 1 August when King Leopold agreed that Prince Baudouin should be *de facto* monarch (though his title was Prince-Royal) until his twenty-first birthday in September 1951. Accordingly Leopold abdicated next year to make way for his son.

The new King, Baudouin, was tall, bespectacled and of a shy and rather retiring disposition. His mother Queen Astrid had been killed in a car crash when he was only three; at the age of nine he had been made a prisoner of the Germans, together with his father; after liberation by the Americans at the end of the war he had shared the royal family's exile in Switzerland; he had returned to a Belgium gripped by crisis and riddled with dissent.

Baudouin's reign got off to an unhappy and uncertain start. In 1952 he declined to attend the funeral of King George VI, sending his brother Albert instead. This lapse in protocol reflected the continuing rift between the House of Windsor and the Belgian royal house, for George VI had regarded King Leopold's wartime activities and alleged pro-German sympathies with considerable displeasure. King Baudouin was attacked in the left-wing Belgian press for his failure to attend the funeral of the dead British King. A year later Baudouin again provoked criticism by his tardy return to Belgium when the worst floods in living memory had devastated large areas of the country, causing the loss of twenty-two lives.

Resentment against King Leopold III lingered on and was fed by his continuing presence at Laeken Palace and by the suspicion that he was unduly influencing his son's political judgement. In May 1959 Leopold helped to remove some of the cause for resentment by announcing that he would no longer live at Laeken and would henceforth devote himself to his hobby of collecting zoological and botanical specimens.

Even the marriages of King Baudouin and his brother Prince Albert aroused criticism. Prince Albert (who married in 1959) had originally announced that he would marry his Italian bride, Donna Paola Ruffo de Calabria, in the Vatican; after protest from anti-clerical factions the wedding took place in Brussels. In 1960 King Baudouin married a Spanish aristocrat, the thirty-two-year-old Doña Fabiola de Mora y Aragon; there was some criticism of the choice of a bride from Franco's Spain. Queen Fabiola has, in fact, proved a pious and politically uncontentious consort, but she has failed to produce an heir and has suffered a number of miscarriages. It seems likely that the eventual successor of Baudouin will be Prince Philippe, the son of Prince Albert and Princess Paola, born on 15 April 1960.

King Baudouin has made considerable headway since the unhappy first decade of his reign. He has reconciled his family with the British royal family, and in 1963 paid a state visit to London. He has seemed reasonably liberal in his political attitudes, and was, for example, believed to have favoured independence for the Congo before his government did. He has attempted to make the Belgian monarchy more informal, has invited groups of students and trade unionists to royal garden parties, and has given press conferences. He is a hard-working monarch who arrives punctually at 9 a.m. to begin work at his Brussels palace. He has survived the chronic Belgian conflict over the claims of the two main language groups (the Flemish and the French-speaking Walloons) as well as the recurring doubts as to whether the nation needs a monarchy at all.

He has built up a considerable popularity despite (or perhaps because of) his ability to exercise a good deal of constitutional power. This is especially evident in his role in appointing a *formateur* to talk to party leaders after a general election and then to report back to him; the King then chooses a statesman to form a government. Because the Belgian system of proportional representation usually fails to produce a one-party government, the part played by the King and the *formateur* after general elections is a particularly important one. On one occasion the King also refused to accept the cabinet's resignation (in 1963 over the language problem), urging instead a solution through further discussion; this provided an eventual compromise. Baudouin's political voice can also be heard on occasion when he sees fit to inform the press of his interpretation of the constitution. There is no doubt, indeed, that this apparently diffident monarch has kept the tradition of active Belgian kingship very much alive.

242 (Left) A frank but subtle postcard portrait of the womanizing King Leopold II of Belgium. During his reign Belgium had a sorry record in the Congo, where some of the worst cruelties of colonial rule took place; Leopold was also unpopular at home.

243 Leopold I of Belgium – Queen Victoria's ambitious Uncle Leopold of Saxe-Coburg, the founder of the Belgian royal family.

244 Queen Elisabeth, wife of Albert I.

245 Albert I of Belgium, diplomatic and tactful, did much to restore the popularity of the monarchy by ruling strictly within the constitution.

246 A 1938 photograph, showing the serious young King Leopold III with his mother, Queen Elizabeth, and a worried-looking President Lebrun.

247 *(Above) Leopold III's wife, Queen Astrid, killed in a*
car crash in 1935. Leopold, who was sitting beside her,
escaped injury.

248 *(Right) The wreck of the car in which Queen Astrid*
met her death.

249 The present King of the Belgians, King Baudouin, was only three when his mother Queen Astrid died; this photograph shows him as a grave little boy at the Laeken Palace, the Belgian royal family's home.

250 (Below) At the Tomb of the Unknown Warrior in Brussels, 1933. Left to right: Prince Leopold (later Leopold III), Queen Elisabeth, King Albert I, Princess Astrid (wife of Leopold), and Prince Charles of the Belgians (Leopold's brother).

251 (Right) Against his ministers' advice Leopold III refused to go into exile on the German invasion in 1940; he advised his troops to surrender, and stayed on as a German prisoner. After the war, the Belgians would not accept Leopold back until 1950. Soon after his return he was forced by public opinion to abdicate in favour of his son, King Baudouin. This photograph, taken 7 July 1951, shows Leopold presenting his son to the people as their new King, on the balcony of the Royal Palace in Brussels.

252 (Above left) Leopold receiving the National League of Veterans at Laeken in 1959. He left Laeken at about this time in deference to criticism that he was too influential with Baudouin.

254 Prince Charles of the Belgians, Leopold's brother, under police protection in 1937, after casting his vote at a polling booth in an industrial area of Brussels.

253 (Below left) The 1950 anti-Leopold riots in Brussels. Note the paving stones ready for use by the rioters.

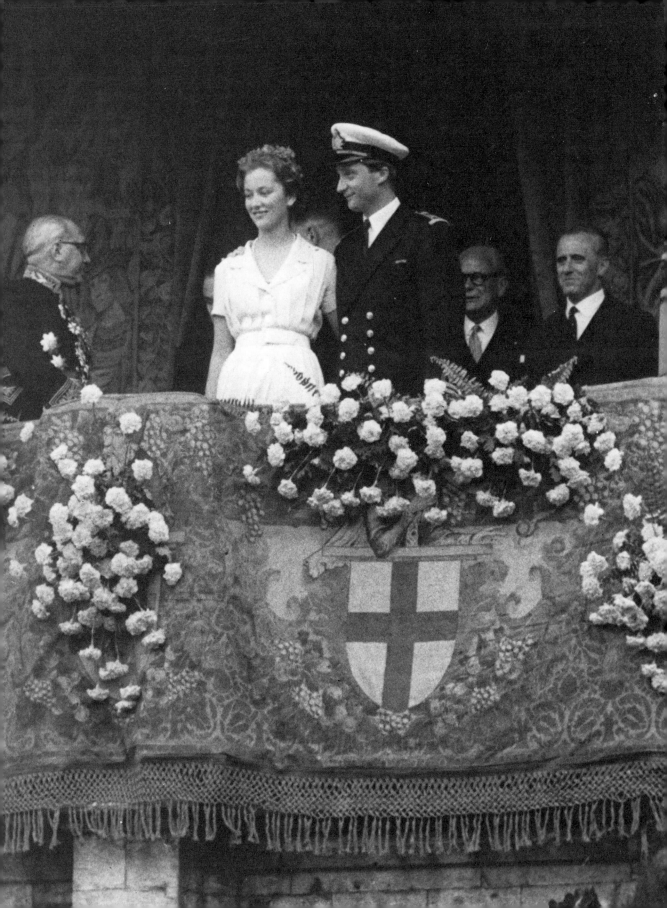

255 (Left) Prince Albert, brother of Baudouin, with his fiancée, Donna Paola Ruffo of Calabria, in 1959. Prince Albert was the next in succession to the throne as King Baudouin was still unmarried.

256 Smiles and roses from King Baudouin greeting his Spanish fiancée, Doña Fabiola de Mora y Aragon, at Brussels Airport in 1960. There was some opposition to Baudouin's choice of a wife from fascist Spain.

257 (Left) Princess Paola and Prince Albert of the Belgians in 1962 with their son Prince Philippe and the baby Princess Astrid. King Baudouin and Queen Fabiola are still childless; therefore Prince Philippe seems likely to succeed to the Belgian throne.

258 King Baudouin at military manoeuvres in 1956, during the first rather unhappy decade of his reign.

259 (Overleaf) Baudouin looks with concern at his bride, Fabiola, as she weeps during their wedding ceremony.

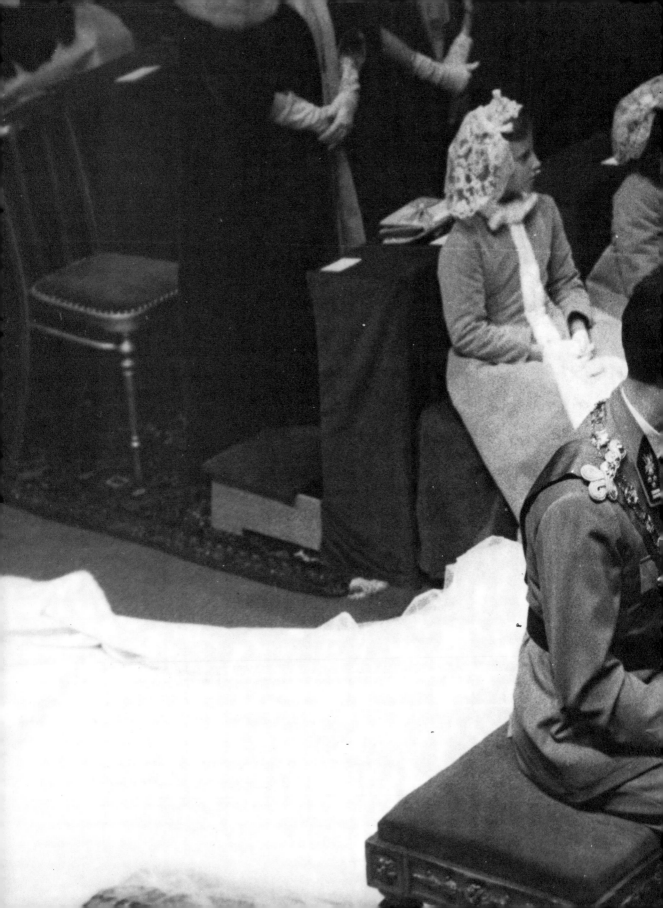

260 *Princess Désirée of Sweden learning child-care in Stockholm. She is one of the four daughters of Crown Prince Gustav Adolf who was killed in a plane crash before inheriting the throne. They are the grand-daughters of Gustav VI. The picture was taken in 1958 when the Princess was 19.*

261 *Princess Christina of Sweden, another of Gustav VI's grand-daughters, wearing a student's white cap and taking part in the celebrations for those matriculating in Stockholm in 1963.*

262 *(Below) Crown Prince Carl Gustav, Gustav VI's grandson, was thrown up in the air by his student friends on matriculating in 1966. In 1973 he became King Carl XVI of Sweden.*

Chapter Seven

The Scandinavian Monarchies

Sweden

The Swedish way of life has been regarded for many decades as an example of efficient, practical, social democratic and egalitarian progress. Yet an aristocracy still exists, and there are millionaires, a House of Nobility in Stockholm, huge private estates – and a monarchy. The Bernadotte dynasty are descendants of Napoleon's marshal Jean Baptiste Bernadotte, who became King Carl XIV in 1818; the Swedish royal family has survived a century and a half of social upheaval, industrialization and democratization, and still occupies part of one of the largest palaces in the world. Though there is a strong republican element in Swedish society it has not yet proved strong enough to sweep away the Bernadottes.

The Swedish throne in the twentieth century has been dominated by two monarchs: Gustav V (1907–50) and Gustav VI Adolf (1950–73). When Gustav V came to the throne he was able to exercise considerable authority; in 1907 only 9·5 per cent of the population could vote, and genuine parliamentary government had only begun in 1905. But by 1918 universal suffrage had been achieved, and by 1917 the constitution had become a proper parliamentary monarchy. This did not, however, prevent Gustav V from interfering in political matters, notably in foreign affairs. King Gustav had married the daughter of the Grand Duke of Baden; his country had a good many close links with Germany; and German was the main foreign language taught in Swedish schools. Gustav made no secret of his pro-German sympathies. Despite some pressure to enter the First World War on Germany's side, Sweden nevertheless remained neutral; in 1939 the Nazi regime evoked far fewer sympathies. Gustav wrote a personal letter to Hitler after the assault on Denmark and Norway assuring the Führer that Sweden would stay neutral during the war and expressing his hopes that there would be no German attack on his country.

Gustav V's pro-German convictions and his occasional constitutional lapses stirred up republican feeling, even though the Social Democrats (who have been almost continually in office since 1932) eventually came to accept the existence of the monarchy. But the chief credit for maintaining the Swedish monarchy as a workable institution belongs to Gustav VI Adolf who succeeded to the throne in 1950 and died in September 1973. Gustav VI had been Crown Prince for forty-three years before he became King. He married twice: his first wife was Princess Margaret of Connaught, a grand-daughter of Queen Victoria, who bore him five children; in 1923 he married Lady Louise Alexandra Mountbatten, a great-grand-daughter of Queen Victoria, the sister of Princess Alice of Greece and Earl Mountbatten, and an aunt of Prince Philip, Duke of Edinburgh. Queen Louise, who died in 1965, was an unpretentious consort who was happy to stroll around Stockholm in ordinary clothes and who described herself as a 'housewife' in the National Health register.

King Gustav VI's marital connections were therefore unreservedly British. His constitutional behaviour also had much more in common with the House of Windsor than with his father. His private interests, moreover, were essentially intellectual and academic; rather than sports cars and horse racing, he preferred archaeology and gardening; he led a number of archaeological expeditions to Italy, Greece, Egypt and China, and was made a member of various illustrious scientific societies – including Britain's Royal Society; he enjoyed browsing in bookshops and sought scholarly solitude whenever he could.

The eldest son of King Gustav, the Crown Prince Gustav Adolf, was killed in a plane crash in 1947. The King's grandson Carl Gustav was made Crown Prince instead, and in 1965, at the age of eighteen, he took, before Parliament, the oath of allegiance to the 'King of Sweden, the Goths and the Wends'. Carl Gustav became Crown Prince because King Gustav VI's second son Prince Bertil was unmarried and unlikely to produce an heir, and his two other sons had married commoners and thus renounced their claims to the throne. In September 1973 the Crown Prince ascended the throne as King Carl XVI amid speculation that he might well be the last Swedish monarch. Gustav VI's daughter Ingrid married the King of Denmark, Frederick IX. His four grand-daughters (progeny of the dead Crown Prince Gustav Adolf) have presented a lively image to their contemporaries: Princesses Margaretha, Birgitta, Désirée and Christina have travelled widely and made marriages across international frontiers. Perhaps the current relationship between the Swedish royal family and their people was best symbolized by the report carried in a Stockholm newspaper that Princess Christina, as she was about to depart for Radcliffe College in Massachusetts, was heading 'for a fun-packed year of good fellowship and collegiate love affairs'.

263 King Gustav's second wife, Queen Louis of Sweden, born the English Lady Louise Mountbatten, talking to a resident in an Old People's Home. 'I will never marry a King or a widower', Louise used to say; her husband was both.

264 (Left) King Gustav VI of Sweden, who reigned from 1950 to 1973, opening the Swedish Riksdag (Parliament) in 1961. He made his speech from the 300-year-old silver throne in the Hall of State in Stockholm.

265 King Gustav VI and Queen Louise just before take-off from Stockholm airport for a European tour in 1952.

266 (Below) Gustav was an enthusiastic archaeologist. This picture, taken in 1962, shows the King hard at work on a site near Manziana in Italy.

267 (Above left) King Gustav VI as Crown Prince with his first wife, also English, Princess Margaret of Connaught. Gustav was Crown Prince for 43 years before becoming King.

268 (Below left) Princess Margaretha of Sweden, the eldest of King Gustav's grand-daughters, on her engagement to Mr John Ambler, a London businessman, in 1964.

269 (Above right) King Oscar II of Sweden with his wife. He was the last King of Sweden who was also King of Norway, for Norway declared itself independent in 1905.

270 (Below right) Princess Birgitta – the first of the royal grand-daughters to become engaged – with her future husband, Prince Johann Georg von Hohenzollern-Sigmaringen, in 1960.

271 (Above, opposite) Gustav VI's father, Gustav V (1907–1950), was pro-German, married to a German, but remained neutral in both the First and Second World Wars. This is an early photograph of the King (second from the right) on an elk-hunting expedition in Värmland in north west Sweden.

272 (Below, opposite) Prince Gustav Adolf of Sweden, riding through Stockholm on his Triumph motor-cycle in the inter-war period. He died in a plane crash.

273 *King Gustav VI giving the Nobel Prize for chemistry to Professor Hermann Standinger of Germany in December* 1953. *This task was clearly congenial to the academic and intellectual King.*

274 Prince Wilhelm of Sweden, Gustav VI's brother, was a professional writer of poetry and travel books. This *photograph was taken in 1959; the Prince bears a marked resemblance to the poet W. H. Auden.* 199

275 *A lithe Princess Birgitta of Sweden, barefooted in a gymnastics class in Stockholm, 1958.*

276 *King Gustav VI and Queen Louise paid a state visit to Britain in June 1954. The picture shows King Gustav, accompanied by the Duke of Edinburgh, inspecting a Guard of Honour.*

277 *King Christian X of Denmark (born 1870 and died 1947), his wife Queen Alexandrine and their sons, Crown Prince Frederik, later Frederik IX (right), and Prince Knud.*

278 *King Christian IX of Denmark (ruled 1863–1906) who was known as 'the grandfather of Europe'. His children were: Frederik VIII of Denmark; George I of Greece; Alexandra, Queen of England; and Dagmar (Marie), Empress of Russia.*

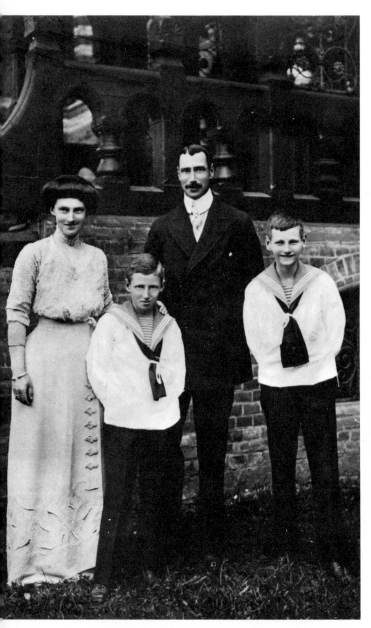

Denmark

The Danish royal house of Oldenborg is the oldest in Europe, dating back to 1448 – before the Wars of the Roses had broken out in England. The blood of the House of Oldenborg has been disseminated throughout the royal families of Europe after centuries of intermarrying. King Christian IX, who ruled from 1863 to 1906, was called 'the grandfather of Europe'; his son became Frederik VIII of Denmark, another son was recruited as King George I of Greece in 1864, his daughter Alexandra became the wife of the future Edward VII of Britain, and another daughter, Dagmar, married Tsar Alexander III of Russia. King Frederik VIII's eldest son became King Christian X and died in 1947. His second son was invited to become King of Norway in 1905 and ruled the country as King Haakon VII until 1957. Christian X was succeeded by his son, Frederik IX, who married Princess Ingrid of Sweden and produced three girls, Margrethe, Benedikte and Anne-Marie.

In 1953 the constitution was amended to allow Princess Margrethe to succeed her father Frederik IX, since previously women had been barred from ascending the throne. One reason why the constitution was thus amended was to bypass King Frederik's somewhat uninspiring brother Prince Knud. In 1972 King Frederik died and was laid to rest in the tenth-century Roskilde Cathedral outside Copenhagen founded by his ancestor Harald Bluetooth, and Margrethe became Queen.

The Danish monarchy's constitutional authority is more apparent than real. Though the constitution states that 'The legislative power shall be vested in the Monarch and the Folketing [parliament] conjointly. The executive power shall be vested in the Monarch,' in fact the monarch rubber-stamps the decisions and policy of the elected government. The monarch must be a member of the Lutheran Church and must also seek parliamentary approval for his or her marriage partner. Democratic, bicycle-riding and unostentatious as the Danish royal family is, however, as long as it exists it will enjoy certain privileges and undertake certain official chores.

King Frederik IX, King of Denmark, of the Wends and the Goths, Duke of Schleswig, Holstein, Stormarn, Ditmarsken, Lauenborg and Oldenborg, was a gigantic (6 foot 4 inches) sportsman, with tattoos, a nautical squint and a passion for good music. His subjects were satisfied, however, that he carried himself like a King. His youngest daughter Anne-Marie became Queen of Greece when her husband Constantine ascended the Greek throne in 1964. His eldest daughter Margrethe married a French diplomat, now entitled Prince Hendrik, and they have two sons Prince Frederik and Prince Joachim.

Queen Margrethe, who like Queen Elizabeth II is a great-great-grand-daughter of Queen Victoria, has been well and variously educated. She went for a time to an English girls' public school near Basingstoke (where 'I was in the top form for three terms and made some very good friends'); she was attached to Girton College, Cambridge, for a year, and also studied sociology at the London School of Economics. She is also engrossed in the study of archaeology and used to accompany her grandfather, King Gustav VI of Sweden, on the Etruscan digs supervised by the Swedish Institute in Rome. Margrethe speaks good English and even better French, which she generally uses when talking to her husband. She is obviously intelligent, strong-minded and serious – though not lacking a sense of humour.

Though Margrethe's life is not by any means hidebound with royal convention, she does accept the need for a degree of protocol, which she feels should not be 'a straitjacket to make people feel uncomfortable. It's a framework to make things easier. For instance fifty people can't go through the same doorway all at once. Someone has to go first.' She also believes that the informality of her royal house owes something to the fact that Denmark is a small country. 'Because we're so small, threads cross each other in a different way. I don't have a fixed set of ideas or principles, I simply play it by ear.' Her husband considers that his position as Prince Consort is 'no worse than if, for instance, a man is married to a woman cabinet minister'. Her subjects would probably prefer her to keep a small but meaningful distance between the throne and themselves, and her role has been described as 'the first among equals' – an appropriate motto for the times.

279 The three Scandinavian Kings during the First World
War: Frederik VIII of Denmark, Gustav V of Sweden,
and Haakon VII of Norway.

280 (Left) The Crown Prince Frederik of Denmark, later King Frederik IX (1947–1973), gigantic, musical, unassuming, conscientious. He loved boats and sailing and would sometimes signal at night in Morse with a torch to the captains of ships passing his royal palace, the Amalienborg, in Copenhagen.

281 Frederik IX, when Crown Prince, taking part in a shooting contest in Copenhagen. He enjoyed outdoor sports and was an excellent shot.

282 (Below) Prince Georg of Denmark and his brother Prince Flemming, the sons of Prince Axel of Denmark, playing at being mechanics with their American toy car.

283 *The Danish royal family in 1952 wearing local clothing during a visit to Greenland. As the King once told his wife, 'I have never found a four-leaf clover, but with the years one has grown up in my home; you, my dear, and our three daughters. The four of you have been the clover leaf that has brought happiness into my life, and sunshine streaming into my heart.'*

284 *(Right) Prince Axel of Denmark, his wife Princess Margarethe and their sons, Georg and Flemming, allegedly laughing at an anti-royalist joke—as well they might, for republicanism hardly exists in Denmark.*

285 (Left) Princess Margrethe, Frederik IX's eldest daughter, now Queen of Denmark, on her way to Cambridge where she spent a year at Girton in 1960.

286 Princess Margrethe in 1967 with her French fiancée, Comte Henri de Montezat, now Prince Hendrik.

287 King Frederik IX and Queen Ingrid saying their
farewells to a haggard King George VI and Queen
Elizabeth after their state visit to London in 1951.

289 (Right) King Frederik feeding the pigeons in St
Mark's Square, Venice, on a private visit to Italy in
October 1956.

288 (Below) In 1957 Queen Ingrid and her daughters
spent an afternoon watching the Duke of Edinburgh playing
polo at Windsor.

290 *Again in England, in 1955, King Frederik was given a warm welcome by the crowds when he came to inspect the Buffs, the Royal East Kent regiment, at Canterbury. The King was honorary Colonel of the Buffs.*

291 *(Right) Princess Margrethe of Denmark apparently out walking with a statue at an exhibition in Copenhagen, 1969.*

Norway

From 1814 to 1905 Norway was united with Sweden under the Swedish crown. In the last years of the nineteenth century the Norwegians began to agitate for complete independence. A constitutional crisis developed in 1905 when King Oscar II vetoed a bill passed by the Norwegian parliament (or Storting) which established a separate consular service in foreign countries; the Norwegian cabinet resigned, and the Storting declared the union dissolved. Eventually the Swedish parliament agreed to accept the dissolution provided a Norwegian plebiscite showed that the people wanted it; in the subsequent voting 368,208 people supported the dissolution of the union while 184 voted against such a move.

Though Norway could have opted for a republic, the throne was eventually offered to Prince Carl of Denmark. A second plebiscite revealed that three-quarters of those who voted favoured Carl, who then ascended the throne as King Haakon VII, thus founding the first Norwegian royal house in six hundred years. Haakon VII died in 1957 at the age of eighty-five; at the time of his death he was the world's oldest and longest-reigning monarch; his wife Queen Maud (a daughter of Edward VII and Queen Alexandra) had died in 1938.

King Haakon's reign was abruptly interrupted by the German conquest of Norway in 1940. In the preceding thirty-five years he had not made himself widely popular; tall, craggy and rather reserved, he had found it difficult to shed his Danish qualities and cultural interests for Norwegian equivalents. The growing strength of the Labour party also provided him with some embarrassment; Norwegian socialism was strongly anti-monarchical, and in the period between the two World Wars Labour leaders had deliberately slighted the King by refusing invitations to dine at the royal palace at the opening of parliamentary sessions; on one occasion the Labour burgomaster of Oslo did not invite Haakon to the laying of the foundation stone of the new town hall, though the King reasonably requested that he might attend as a subscriber to the building fund. In all, the King did nothing to antagonize the Labour party, offering them their first taste of power in 1928 and accepting their rise to a thirty years' supremacy in 1935.

Republican agitation continued, however, during these years. It was Haakon's brave stand against the German invaders that gave the monarchy its greatest boost in popularity. He would not let his government capitulate and refused to appoint the fascist Vidkun Quisling to the premiership as Hitler demanded; instead, the government and the royal family moved to the far north of the country. At last in June 1940, two months after the invasion, Haakon and his ministers escaped to Britain, where they set up a government-in-exile and established the Free Norwegian forces. After helping to inspire and co-ordinate Norway's heroic contribution to the defeat of the Axis powers, Haakon returned to his country on 7 June 1945 to a rapturous reception as the monarch who had not surrendered his nation's honour.

In 1957 Crown Prince Olav succeeded his father as King Olav V, after a fifty-two-year stretch as heir to the throne. Born in England before his father accepted the Norwegian crown, Olav was sent to an ordinary secondary school and then to Norway's Military College; his further education was completed by reading international law and politics at Balliol College, Oxford. In 1928 Olav won a gold medal as a yachtsman at the Amsterdam Olympic Games, and he also excelled at other outdoor activities. During the war he helped to lead Norway's resistance to the German invasion, and in London he was Commander-in-

Chief of the Free Norwegian forces. Olav married Princess Martha of Sweden (who died in 1954) and fathered a son (Prince Harald) and two daughters; Crown Prince Harald has one son and one daughter. Olav's fluent Norwegian and his thoroughly Norwegian up-bringing were in inevitable contrast to his father's Danish background. When he became King he lived unostentatiously and gave the impression of an earnest monarch anxious to do his duty with as much efficiency and as little display as possible.

The Norwegian crown can only be passed to a male heir. The constitution theoretically concentrates executive power in the hands of the King and the Council of State (the Cabinet), but, as in other Scandinavian monarchies, the monarch merely gives his formal assent to the proposals of the Council of State. The Norwegian people would not tolerate any unconstitutional behaviour on the part of their sovereign, and the King can ask search-ing questions of his ministers but not really question their decisions. The Norwegian monarchy will presumably not outlive its usefulness; to date it has provided a modest and sometimes inspiring service to the nation, and as long as this rapport is maintained its future will be secure. But it is, after all, a comparatively new institution, and Scandinavians have enjoyed repeating the story of the Dane who emigrated to Norway and soon became one of the country's biggest hotel owners; one day he was formally introduced to King Haakon, who said, 'I am pleased to meet a Dane who has done so well in Norway', to which the successful businessman replied, 'And the same to you, your Majesty.'

293 King Haakon VII of Norway (1905–1957), on a
visit to Stockholm in 1953, in animated conversation with
King Gustav VI of Sweden. The King took the name of
Haakon when he accepted the Norwegian throne in 1905.
In the Second World War, he refused to capitulate and was
an inspiration to the Norwegian Resistance – perhaps his
chief achievement.

294 Crown Prince Olav, the son of King Haakon and
Queen Maud, with his wife, Martha of Sweden, who died
in 1954. Prince Olav succeeded his father as Olav V in
1957, after being heir to the throne for 52 years. During the

German occupation of Norway, Prince Olav helped to lead
the Resistance and was Commander-in-Chief of the Free
Norwegian forces in London.

295 (Below) The christening of Crown Prince Olav's son,
Prince Harald, in 1937. Only males can succeed to the
Norwegian throne, so the birth of Harald was of great
significance. Queen Maud is standing on the left; the tall
central figure in the back row is King Haakon. Crown
Prince Olav, covered with decorations, stands behind his wife
Princess Martha, who is seated holding the little Prince,
with her daughters, Princess Ragnhild and Princess Astrid,
on either side.

296 (Above left) King Haakon and Queen Maud, with Crown Prince Olav and Princess Martha on their way to dinner at the Royal Yacht Club in Oslo, 1938. There was little ceremony about their lives. Queen Maud once exclaimed, 'I am so glad that I am Queen of a country in which everybody loves simplicity.'

297 (Below left) An elk-hunting party in 1954 in south-west Sweden. Left to right: Crown Prince Olav of Norway, a forester, King Frederik IX of Denmark and his younger brother Prince Wilhelm. It is interesting to compare this picture with the photograph of Gustav V of Sweden's hunting party (no. 271).

298 In 1969 King Olaf V of Norway met King Constantine of Greece at the Royal Thames Yacht Club in London where they attended a meeting of the International Yacht Racing Union's Olympic Committee. In 1928 King Olav won a gold medal as a yachtsman in the Amsterdam Olympic Games.

299 King Haakon and Crown Prince Olav in London, 1940, at the Norway Relief Depot in Cadogan Square. Their courage was an inspiration to Norwegians, who resisted the Nazi invasion with great heroism.

300 *King Haakon in 1957 shortly before his death at 85, after a reign of 52 years.*

301 When a prince falls in love it is a matter of public
concern even in the 1970s. Crown Prince Harald and Sonja
Haraldsen appeared to enjoy the interest taken in the progress
of their courtship. And by fathering two children since their
marriage in 1972 Harald has at least contributed
something to the perpetuation of the monarchy.